Praise for *Gluten-Free in Five Minutes*

"Whether you are a seasoned chef or new to the world of gluten-free cooking, this cookbook is fun and makes it possible to prepare many family favorites at a fraction of the usual time."　　　　　　　　*—Tucson Citizen*

"*Gluten-Free in Five Minutes* is a must-have cookbook for the gluten-free kitchen, especially when the most valuable resource is time."

—Technorati.com

"[S]ome recipes will be especially delightful for those who cannot tolerate gluten, such as two different ones for chocolate pound cake (one using brown rice flour, the other using sorghum flour; there are similar dual recipes for red velvet cake, carrot cake, and regular chocolate cake)."　　　*—InfoDad.com*

"If you're looking for a recipe book with quick, easy recipes, give it a try."

—TheBakingBeauties.com

"An easy-to-use cookbook . . . [with] colorful photographs sure to entice even those who can eat gluten."　　　　　*—San Francisco Book Review*

"Even if you learn to depend on only one or two things, it would be worth the price. We bet you'll find a lot more than that."　　　*—Gluten-Free Living*

"Offers very easy options that can be prepared in minutes. Very highly recommended!"　　　　　　　　　　*—Midwest Book Review*

"This cookbook is ideal for those who'd rather not spend time over a hot stove, and we're thinking it's great for college-age kids with no access to a fully equipped kitchen. The scope is wide, the steps are few, the work is quick. And the results speak for themselves."　　　　*—Living Without*

"For those of us (with kids or not) who like to experiment and play around in the kitchen with some simple ingredients, and who like the idea of whipping up something homemade in a few minutes, this is a really fun gluten-free cookbook. I recommend it."　　　　　　　　*—About.com*

"All you need is a bowl, a fork, and the microwave to whip up tasty gluten-free cakes, breads, pizza crusts, rolls, and more."　　　*—Taste for Life*

"*Gluten-Free in Five Minutes* provides easy-to-use gluten-free recipes for the microwave. A great book for busy mums or college kids who don't have the luxury of time or a big kitchen but still want to enjoy the luxury of 'home-cooked' food."   —Curled Up with a Good Book, curledup.com

"[A] favorite cookbook of 2011. . . . What sets this gluten-free cookbook apart are its quick and easy recipes for perpetually busy people. This go-to manual for health-conscious cooks on-the-go includes 123 rapid recipes for bread, rolls, cakes, muffins, and more, each designed to fit into hectic lifestyles and delicious enough for the whole family—no matter how busy!"
                    —*Natural Solutions*

You Still Won't Believe It's Gluten-Free!

Also by Roben Ryberg

The Gluten-Free Kitchen

You Won't Believe It's Gluten-Free!

Gluten-Free in Five Minutes

The Ultimate Gluten-Free Cookie Book

Eating for Autism (contributing food writer)

You *Still* Won't Believe It's Gluten-Free!

200 More Delicious, Foolproof Recipes
You and Your Whole Family Will Love

ROBEN RYBERG

Da Capo

LIFE
LONG

A Member of the Perseus Books Group

Production and design by Eclipse Publishing Services and Jill Shaffer
Set in 12-point Chaparral Light by Eclipse Publishing Services

Cataloging-in-Publication data for this book is available from the Library of Congress.

First Da Capo Press edition 2013
ISBN: 978-0-7382-1669-0

Published by Da Capo Press
A Member of the Perseus Books Group
www.dacapopress.com

Note: The information in this book is true and complete to the best of our knowledge. This
book is intended only as an informative guide for those wishing to know more about health
issues. In no way is this book intended to replace, countermand, or conflict with the advice
given to you by your own physician. The ultimate decision concerning care should be made
between you and your doctor. We strongly recommend you follow his or her advice. Information in this book is general and is offered with no guarantees on the part of the authors
or Da Capo Press. The authors and publisher disclaim all liability in connection with the use
of this book. The names and identifying details of people associated with events described in
this book have been changed. Any similarity to actual persons is coincidental.

Da Capo Press books are available at special discounts for bulk purchases in the U.S.
by corporations, institutions, and other organizations. For more information, please contact the Special Markets Department at the Perseus Books Group, 2300 Chestnut Street,
Suite 200, Philadelphia, PA, 19103, or call (800) 810-4145, ext. 5000, or e-mail
special.markets@perseusbooks.com.

10 9 8 7 6 5 4 3 2 1

To those that love me back

Contents

Photographs appear following page 100

Foreword

Roben Ryberg's book, *You Still Won't Believe It's Gluten-Free,* is a wonderful compilation of "out-of-the-box" recipes, delicious and healthy flours, advice for creating a safe gluten-free kitchen, and practical tips for managing a delicious gluten-free lifestyle. While there are increasing numbers of books that cater to people with gluten intolerance, there are only a handful of books on the market that provide information of the quality and range found in *You Still Won't Believe It's Gluten-Free.* Roben's book provides a wonderful way for both adults and children to enjoy a gluten-free diet in a fun, creative way.

Many people worldwide have adopted a gluten-free diet. For those with celiac disease or gluten sensitivity, this diet can be life-saving. Others simply find that the relief from gastrointestinal or neurological symptoms makes their lives much more comfortable.

Gluten intolerance is manifested in several forms, as celiac disease, dermatitis herpetiformis, or DH, or gluten intolerance without celiac disease. *Gluten* is the term for the storage protein of wheat. There are similar proteins, to which people with celiac disease react, found in rye and barley. As a result, the latter two grains are included in the grains to be avoided when an individual is on a gluten-free diet. All other grains are tolerated by over 99 percent of those with celiac disease.

The normal human digestive system does not fully digest gluten; it does not break down gluten as thoroughly as other proteins, leaving large amino acid fragments. In genetically predisposed people, these fragments trigger an inflammatory response in the small intestine that causes villous atrophy and celiac disease. This mechanism is more fully described in the book I coauthored, *Celiac Disease: A Hidden Epidemic*, published by HarperCollins. The mechanism of nonceliac gluten sensitivity has not as yet been described.

Celiac disease is a lifelong, unique autoimmune illness. It occurs in about 1 percent of the population worldwide. There is little knowledge among physicians about the subtle clinical presentations, use of serologic testing, and long-term management. Those with celiac disease require advice and counseling about nutritious and varied substitutes for gluten, similar to the ingredients described in this book, assessment and monitoring of their health and nutrition status, and good medical follow-up for their disease for those with celiac disease have an increased burden of disease compared to the general population. Patients often get no or inadequate medical follow-up. This compares dramatically with the health care systems in most European countries where celiac disease is regarded as a common and important condition.

In contrast to the general prevalence of this disease, there is little medical support for those with celiac disease in the United States. Over the last few years only a few university medical centers have developed specific celiac disease centers like the Celiac Disease Center at Columbia University in New York City.

The Celiac Disease Center at Columbia University provides comprehensive medical care for adults and pediatric patients with celiac disease, including nutrition and attention to the multiple associated conditions that occur in celiac disease. The Center is involved in the care of thousands of patients with celiac disease and gluten intolerance, providing better access to proper testing, diagnosis, treatment, and follow-up care. Celiac disease is a lifelong, unique autoimmune illness that occurs in about 1 percent of the population, worldwide.

All of the Center's research is directed toward celiac disease and reflects the nature of celiac disease as a multisystem disease, including cardiovascular disease, cancer, thyroid disease, infertility, and psychiatric and behavior problems in childhood. Additional information is available online at www.celiacdiseasecenter.org.

It is only with good, ongoing medical care and great attention to a varied and nutritious diet that an adequate quality of life can be maintained.

The entity of gluten intolerance in the absence of celiac disease is more problematic for physicians to deal with. Surprising that something could be more difficult than celiac disease itself! It is more problematic than celiac disease because there is nothing a physician can measure or quantitate in order to assess the patient's disease burden. This compares to celiac disease where we measure antibody levels, assess intestinal biopsy status, and measure vitamin and mineral levels as well as bone density. Gluten intolerance is the reporting of patients that they feel better or symptoms resolve when gluten is withdrawn from the diet.

Dermatitis herpetiformis, or DH, is a manifestation of gluten intolerance that can be assessed. It is diagnosed by skin biopsy, although special studies are required for the biopsy. It is an intensely itchy, usually blistering rash. A very strict gluten-free diet is the mainstay of treatment. While the drug dapsone may be used to control the lesions, it is the diet that prevents the disease and reduces the risk of the development of lymphoma, a known risk of the disease.

Celiac disease and gluten intolerance are great examples of why we need to know what we are eating. This is something that is increasingly difficult in this day and age when food is often grown far from where we live and is made more complicated with the prevalence of processed foods, fast foods, and food additives. Roben's book helps in that she selects simple, readily available, gluten-free ingredients for her "out of the box" fabulous recipes that allow everyone to make gluten-free homemade meals from scratch.

There is no doubt that resources such as this book, *You Still Won't Believe It's Gluten-Free*, are an important adjunct to any household that is attempting to be gluten-free. I congratulate Roben on her superb effort. Read the book and enjoy the delicious gluten-free recipes!

Peter H.R. Green, MD
Professor of Clinical Medicine, Columbia University
Director, Celiac Disease Center at Columbia University
www.celiacdiseasecenter.org

Acknowledgments

Where do you begin when you want to thank people who help you do what you do better?

First and foremost, I need to thank the users of my books. I value your feedback greatly! Yours are the voices that bounce in my head.

To my dearest friends, including my online friends. You have eaten, and eaten, and eaten. You have tested recipes. You've sat at my kitchen counter. You've come for dinner and insisted I prepare gluten-free meals because you know I'm writing. You have nudged and sometimes even pushed me. Although you are many in number, I should name a kitchen stool after my dear friend, Eileen. I am grateful for each of you. Stacie, Cassandra, Jan. I have no words, but know I am so grateful for your ongoing support of my work.

To my food-scientist friend, Sara. You give me the scientific explanation behind my food-science discoveries. I do what I do because my bouncing takes me there. You explain why it works and tell me "you're better than you know."

To my kids. You are amazing. I'm proud to be called your mom.

Introduction

◆

Do you have a favorite neighborhood diner or bar that has especially good food? Maybe a little Thai or Chinese place that's just a little out of the way? It is these restaurants that tempt my palate again and again. Such restaurants are the inspiration for these recipes. They offer fast, delicious food with a nod to healthful, and they never sacrifice flavor.

No home kitchen, restaurant, bar, or catered event is safe from my scrutiny. I will shamelessly ask the chef for a little sauce "to go." I will beg family secrets. I will eat plate after plate of delicious food so that I may be inspired to replicate dishes for you.

You may wonder why I work with gluten-free foods when I am not gluten-free. My interest began with a simple request from a friend with celiac disease who desperately wanted something good to eat, and it continues because I am a foodie who loves food science. Who better to taste and analyze delicious gluten-filled foods and then recreate them gluten-free? It is a win–win, whether recreating great fakes of Girl Scout cookies*, perfecting onion rings, or trying that new dish that a friend talked about!

*See *The Ultimate Gluten-Free Cookie Book* also by Roben Ryberg.

Gluten-free food science is developing every day. I'm proud to be a part of that science. I was the first, and maybe still am, the only gluten-free food writer who works with just one flour at a time. Walking away from the "tower of flours" is liberating! *You Won't Believe It's Gluten-Free* was groundbreaking in that way. With the passing of the "cardboard gluten-free food era," no one had imagined using just one flour to successfully create delicious gluten-free foods.

You Still Won't Believe It's Gluten-Free carries on that tradition—but more so. In this book, we dive into amazing breads, perhaps the best I have ever formulated. We enjoy more diverse cuisine. We enjoy moist textures in baked goods. And, we do it all with two of my favorite whole-grain flours, brown rice and sorghum.

Creating new food theory is hard work—fun, challenging, and ultimately delicious but still hard work. I am delighted that it is my job to do so.

You may be wondering, more specifically, what makes my recipes different from those of other gluten-free chefs.

1. I don't use flour blends.

During the early days of gluten-free baking, many recipes would utilize a cup-for-cup substitution for all-purpose wheat flour in recipes. Rice flour was one popular choice. This approach was easy and affordable, but unfortunately it created terrible, cardboard-like food.

Another approach was to combine a variety of flours to mimic the texture of traditional all-purpose wheat flour. It really was a great concept! All-purpose wheat flour is perfect for baking; it's not too light, not too heavy. It is the standard, the forbidden, can't-eat-it standard!

By comparison rice flour and cornmeal are heavy. Potato starch is light, and tapioca starch is lighter yet! Bean flour has medium weight and good protein. The idea is that if you take a couple of heavies, add in a couple of lights, throw in a little higher protein, you have a cup-for-cup substitute for all-purpose wheat flour. You still have the issues of binders, moisture retention, extra eggs, and maybe a little tweaking, but you have something that lives in the same neighborhood as wheat flour.

In my view, there are a few disadvantages to this approach. First, you end up with a "tower of flours." You have spent a lot of money stocking your pantry. You are giving a "sensitive" immune system, two, four, or even more flours to substitute for wheat. Most importantly, some of these blends contain one or more flours that are among the top allergens in the United States. Focusing on this allergen connection (on top of the gluten intolerance) was, for me, a "light-bulb" moment. Could we abandon blends? While I respectfully confirm that blends can be quite tasty and used successfully in baking, they are simply not necessary.

I've heard the comment that "you can't make good gluten-free foods without blends." And that makes me sad. It is only because of minds open to new food theory that angel food cake, chiffon cake, or even chocolate chip cookies were invented! We have no ancient bakers to tell us how to make the very best gluten-free foods. We are the scientists!

2. I embrace the unique characteristics of each flour.

Cup-for-cup doesn't cut it when using just one gluten-free flour! You must embrace each flour's individual flavors and baking characteristics. In gluten-free baking, just a little difference in measurement can make a big difference in results, especially when using just one flour at a time. But if we treat a banana like a banana, an orange like an orange, or a cup of rice flour like a cup of rice flour, we can simplify our baking and reveal the secrets and subtleties of each flour.

3. I use whole-grain flours.

There was a time I thought baking with whole grains would yield gritty textures or overly strong flavors. Not so. It's all about common sense and appropriate formulations. If you need mild flavor, use a mild-tasting flour. If robust flavor is needed, use a stronger-tasting flour.

4. I love moisture retention.

The simple order in which ingredients are combined makes a huge difference in how long a cake or bread stays moist. That discovery is huge! It means you can bake a cake or bread, leave it on the counter for several days, and still enjoy that perfect food!

I recall the days when extra servings of baked goods needed to be stored in the freezer (or fridge at minimum) to delay crumbling and drying. Then, of course, you had to microwave a serving briefly, and perhaps even toast it to make it palatable. It seems almost funny today.

5. I champion affordability.

We can, and do, achieve incredible results with simple, everyday ingredients. In the recipes in this book, I use brown rice flour, sorghum flour, and sometimes white rice flour (for the most delicate cakes). All of these flours are affordable, readily available, and do a GREAT job. Specialty ingredients are kept to a minimum.

6. I think food should taste good.

Many years ago, I recall that foods were considered "good for being gluten-free." Fortunately, that time has long passed; there is no need for such a qualifier. Gluten-free foods are just plain good. Truly, the food in this book will WOW you. The recipes are that good. The breads are that good! I am beyond pleased to share them with you.

The gluten-free industry has changed so much over the years. It's gone from cardboard to gourmet! It moved from single-grains to blends! And for me, for us, it switched from blends to single grains!

Think of the pendulum that swung too far in one direction. Our food answers lie right here in the middle, right before us. Simple is best. Existing, affordable flours do the job well! Single, whole-grain formulations are amazing.

So, whether you have 20 minutes to throw together dinner, need a special celebration cake, or want something wonderful to share at a family picnic, you and I are likely on the same page. Some things do not change in my work. My recipes make food that is easy to prepare, delicious, and affordable. And just as with *You Won't Believe It's Gluten-Free!*, if it's not good enough for every-one, it's not in this book.

Let me show you that "You still won't believe it's gluten-free!"

CHAPTER 1

Kitchen and Baking

◆

Getting a diagnosis of celiac disease or gluten intolerance can be shocking to anyone! But it also offers an incredible opportunity to achieve wellness. The journey to diagnosis is often long and frustrating. Treatment is simple, but it is not easy: Remove gluten from your diet. You may also need to avoid other foods, like dairy, at least for a while. We will start by spring-cleaning your kitchen, or at least a cabinet and a counter or two.

Note: For those of you already familiar with creating a safe gluten-free kitchen, this information may be a bit redundant.

Creating a Safe Gluten-Free Kitchen

It's probably most convenient to make your kitchen a gluten-free zone. Some come to that decision immediately; some come to that decision eventually; and some just carve out a safe space within their kitchens or banish gluten to the garage or basement.

Whether you're removing gluten from the whole kitchen or just part, the procedures are the same.

1. Remove gluten-containing ingredients and those that may have been cross-contaminated with gluten. Cross-contamination can occur when any "forbidden" grain or flour (or something made with such) comes in contact with a gluten-free food.

    Labeling of unsafe ingredients has improved as the Food and Drug Administration has worked to regulate labeling of top allergens in the United States. Generally speaking, this makes wheat easy to find on the ingredients label. You must also remove rye, barley, spelt, kamut, and unsafe oats (many are cross-contaminated in transport, storage, and processing). Malt may be an issue as well. It is easiest to just avoid it.

    Look closely at condiments, too. Soy sauce and spice mixes often contain wheat. And cross-contamination can be a real issue for condiments. The mayonnaise or margarine in your refrigerator may have been cross-contaminated by a knife used in preparing traditional sandwiches. It matters. If you share your kitchen with others, consider using a separate mini-fridge, separate shelf, or even colored dots to designate the items you alone must use. There is also a possibility for cross-contamination during production of food items. Many manufacturers have gone to great lengths to provide you with the safest possible foods. Should you have ongoing difficulties, though, you may need to research how your foods were produced as well.

    If you are in doubt about a food product, look to one of the local or online groups (see the Appendix) for help. Most manufacturers are helpful, too. Zero tolerance of gluten is the plan. There are many wonderful people who will help you achieve it!

    You must develop a plan that works for you. You must keep your food safe.

2. Remove any small appliances that may have residual gluten. Toasters are a crumb-trap. A new "gluten-free only" toaster or waffle iron is a beautiful thing. If an appliance cannot be adequately (meticulously)

cleaned, please do not use it. It takes only a small amount of gluten to cause damage (not to mention making you feel ill). You cannot be nice and "share" your gluten-free toaster. You can, however, share your gluten-free toast!

3. Starting high, then working low, clean out and wash down every surface! I don't know how it happens, but I have crumbs in my silverware drawer. I also have crumbs in my bowl drawer. I'm sure it's because of their proximity to the counter, but even up high, packages leak. Clean, clean, clean. Soap, water, and a fresh dishcloth are perfect for this task.

4. Evaluate everything you cook with and eat from before placing it back into a cabinet. If a baking pan has forever spots on it, take the time to scrub it clean, or always use a piece of foil to line it before use. If you have wooden spoons that you regularly use to stir morning oatmeal (cross-contaminated), splurge on new ones or use a large metal spoon instead.

5. Check your kitchen washables. Wash all towels, aprons, and hot mitts.

6. Replace your unsafe foods with safe foods. It can be overwhelming to think of the expense, but it is critical that you remove foods that are not acceptable in your gluten-free diet. I suggest replacing condiments, pastas, and cereals first. And as you begin to make new recipes, fill those empty cabinets with staples used often in this book, like brown rice flour, sorghum flour, xanthan gum, tomato paste, etc. Just peruse a few recipes before you go shopping!

7. Talk with your family and/or roommates. They are a major factor in keeping your food safe. These common sense suggestions will become second nature with time, but it will be hard to change gears at first. Keep at it, and it will be rewarding for all of you, as a healthier person is a happier person.

   a) Keep a separate counter or use a fresh piece of foil or waxed paper for your prep surface.

b) Avoid flying wheat. Do not be in the same room when someone is mixing up a batch of cookies or making homemade bread. You don't want to inhale the tiny particles. (Make some great gluten-free cookies or bread together instead!)

c) Fix your plate first or from the uncontaminated extras in the kitchen.

d) Keep gluten foods far, far away from gluten-free foods (i.e., finding cracker crumbs on a cheese plate is bad). Again, a separate gluten-free counter or table really should be considered the bare minimum.

e) Make entire meals gluten-free if possible.

Roben's Pantry

Here's a basic list of items you'll want to keep on hand. Most of the products are readily available at your local grocery store. On occasion, I purchase a few items at oriental markets, farmers' markets, and health food stores. There are also plenty of great resources online.

Flours

Brown Rice Flour. Generally speaking, I use Bob's Red Mill. It has a consistent quality and is widely available.

Cornmeal. I have used assorted brands. All have performed well. Cornmeal is used in just a few recipes in this book.

Cornstarch or Potato Starch. I have used assorted brands. All have performed well. Cornstarch or potato starch is used minimally in this book.

Sorghum Flour. I have a history of using Bob's Red Mill. It has a consistent quality and is widely available.

White Rice Flour. Generally speaking, I use Bob's Red Mill. It has a consistent quality and is widely available. I have had success with other brands of white rice flour as well. White rice flour has been used in several of the more delicate recipes in this book.

Other Preferred Ingredients

Baking Powder. Baking powders have different baking properties: Some are more active in the bowl, and others are more active during baking. Rumford is the only baking powder I use. Should other brands be used, the quantity needed may (or may not) need to be adjusted downward by 20 percent.

Baking Soda. I use Arm & Hammer brand. It is widely available.

Butter. I use any brand of lightly salted butter. Annato is a coloring sometimes used to enhance the yellow color of butter. It is gluten-free but not tolerated by everyone.

Cocoa Powder. Please use Hershey's if possible, as recipes have fared better with its use over other brands.

Cream Cheese. Philadelphia is my favorite brand.

Eggs. Use any brand of large eggs. It is important to use size large for consistent results. Please note that sometimes "large" eggs seem quite huge. I believe manufacturers sometimes upsize when they have excess quantities of larger eggs. For our purposes, consistency ensures good results.

Half and Half. Use any brand.

Milk. Use any brand of 2 percent milk. Almond milk and buttermilk have been used in a few recipes as well. Be sure to read the ingredients list before purchase.

Oil. I generally use canola oil, but any mild-tasting vegetable oil should do just fine. Sometimes I use olive oil for its delicious flavor.

Pasta. Tinkyada is my favorite brand. Nothing else has come close for me.

Salt. Use any brand. Iodized salt should be avoided with the DH (skin) presentation of celiac disease.

Spices, Flavorings, and Extracts. McCormick's is my favorite brand. Always check labels for offending ingredients. I usually prefer extracts to flavorings for better taste. Distilled alcohol is considered safe for the gluten-free diet.

Sugar—White, Brown, and Confectioners'. Use any brand. Note that confectioners' sugar sometimes contains cornstarch. Cornstarch is fine for the gluten-free diet but not for the corn-free diet.

Xanthan Gum. I use Bob's Red Mill. It has a consistent quality and is widely available. If you require a substitute for xanthan gum, try guar gum instead, provided the food is baked in a pan for form. Xanthan has more viscosity in the bowl. Guar (as generally available to us) provides more structure during baking, meaning it doesn't thicken as much in the bowl. Substitute 1¼ teaspoons guar gum for each 1 teaspoon of xanthan gum.

Yogurt. Use any brand. I use plain low-fat yogurt. I strongly believe low-fat yogurt performs better in recipes than its nonfat counterpart.

Specialty Items

I have used some wonderful specialty items in this book. They include fermented black beans (packaged in a cardboard cylinder), lemon grass, and bean paste to name a few. None of these ingredients are expensive when purchased at an Asian market. They are delightful additions that diversify the palate. I hope you will venture out to try these as well!

Shopping

A trip to the grocery store will become a new adventure. Generally speaking, if you stick to the outside aisles, most items will be gluten-free. Inside aisles of mixes and prepared foods are trickier. As always, be sure to check labels to make sure any packaged foods you're buying are gluten-free. Here's a basic trip through the grocery store with notes for you on which sections are safest.

Fresh Fruits and Vegetables. Perfect. Enjoy the diversity, but approach any mixes or prepared items carefully.

Deli. Suspect. Check ingredients lists carefully. Obviously macaroni salad is out, but other things may be as well. Some prepared lunch meats are totally fine. Check out the ingredients labels, and find the ones that work for you.

Salad Bar. Provided there is no cross-contamination, enjoy! The salad bar is a great place to pick up ready-chopped ingredients for recipes. Make friends with your deli person if cross-contamination is an issue. The store wants happy customers and should be willing to address your concerns. Croutons would be an obvious source of cross-contamination, but you must look further. For example, a spoon in a pasta salad or even some potato salads can be an issue.

Bakery. Walk on, unless there is a gluten-free section, and then be extremely cautious because baking environments are notorious for "flying" wheat flour dust.

Meats. Enjoy this section of the market. Although most meats have an added solution, I've yet to find any "added solutions" that conflict with a gluten-free diet. But while problems are rare, not every piece of meat or poultry is safe. Read the ingredients list! Any spice or gravy packets that are included should be avoided if you cannot read the ingredients list carefully.

Dairy and Juices. I have yet to find a dairy or juice drink with gluten. That said, you must still read the labels to be safe. Anything that is not 100% juice or 100% milk should be checked closely. Cheeses are wonderful. I do caution, however, as I have found cottage cheese with gluten.

Eggs. Enjoy.

Frozen Foods. Simple frozen vegetables and juices are usually fine. Be careful in purchasing anything with a sauce. Avoid all pastas, pizzas, and sandwiches unless they are specifically labeled as gluten-free. Most ice creams and sorbets should be fine. Just check the labels and be especially watchful for added bits, like cookie dough, that would be prohibited.

Canned Foods. Generally speaking, plain vegetables are safe. Read the labels.

Pasta aisle. Avoid all pastas, except for those labeled as gluten-free. Plain rices, lentils, and beans are fine. Read labels of all mixes carefully. Pasta sauces are often found near the pasta. You have to read the labels. Not all will be safe. Be sure to grab a few basic ingredients for our pasta

Kitchen and Baking

recipes. It takes just a little time and a few ingredients to make your own delicious pasta dishes.

Baking. Except for gluten-free baking ingredients, avoid this aisle. Cake mixes, bread mixes, and muffin mixes are all unacceptable to the gluten-free diet unless specifically labeled otherwise.

Tea/Coffee. Most of these will be fine. Again, read ingredients to be sure.

Cereal. Gluten-free cereals are now available in many grocery stores. Some Chex and Rice Krispies cereals are gluten-free. This is an area where malt and/or factory production can be an issue. Look for gluten-free labeling. Avoid brands of oatmeal that are not specifically labeled gluten-free. Cross-contamination is a serious issue for most oatmeal.

Snacks. Keep walking, except for gluten-free crackers and cookies. Gluten-free crackers may also be kept near the specialty cheese section of the market. Some gluten-free crackers are wonderful!

Candy. Indulge if you must, but read the labels.

Tools in Roben's Kitchen

I moved to a beautiful little house with a very small kitchen a few years ago. It has made me think hard about the things I keep in my kitchen. I've come to realize you don't need fancy appliances or a ton of gadgets to make wonderful food.

Baking Pans. For the basics, you will need cookie sheets, 8x4-inch loaf pan, 8-inch round cake pans, a square cake pan, cupcake pans, and a pie plate. If you want to make wedding and special occasion cakes, you'll need wedding cake pans (6", 8", 10", 12").

COOKIE SHEETS are used for baking cookies and making breads. I love to plop bread dough in the middle of a cookie sheet, shape it, and toss it in the oven. It has become my standard for bread baking.

LOAF PANS are used for making quick breads and loaf breads. My 8x4-inch pan is larger at the top and reduces slightly at its base.

ROUND CAKE PANS are used for almost every cake in this book. My pans are made by Wilton and are a full 1½ inches in height. The additional height provides nice support for the recipes in this book. I consider the ones with very low sides (1 inch) to be too low and prone to overflow.

SQUARE CAKE PANS are used for cakes, rolls, and bar-type cookies. This size pan is not essential if you use a round pan instead.

CUPCAKE PANS are used for muffins and cupcakes. Many recipes make 9 or 10 muffins. I have a single pan that has room for 12.

PIE PLATE. If you make pies, this is pretty important. A standard 9-inch size should be just fine. I prefer Pyrex.

SPRINGFORM PAN. I happen to have a 9-inch springform pan, as well as several mini pans. They are wonderful for tarts. You could, however, just shape the base dough on a cookie sheet and forgo the special pans.

WEDDING CAKE PANS are essential for making wedding cake layers. There is no substitute for the right-size pans. Mine are made by Wilton, and they are perfect for the job. I do not buy the extra-tall Wilton pans; their standard pans (1½ inches tall) are fine.

Bowls. Most any mixing bowl will do. My favorite is an old Tupperware mixing bowl that has a handle and a pour spout. It even has a lid with a hole in the middle of it, which allows the mixer to be used with little regard for splatter. I use a Pyrex bowl for microwaving when needed.

Blender. Cuisinart's stick blender is absolutely wonderful. It should also be used with great care, as the extraordinarily sharp blades continue to spin after the button is released.

Bread Machine. I do not use a bread machine. It is absolutely not necessary for any recipes in any of my books.

Cooling Racks. Cooling racks are especially nice when making cookies; they're great to cool breads and cakes as well.

Cutting Boards. Rubber or soft plastic cutting boards continue to be my favorite. I can scrub them and toss them in the dishwasher without concern.

Deep Fryer. I have a small deep fryer that plugs into the wall. It is very simple to use and does a great job. While it's not an essential item, several recipes in this book really benefit from the ease of using a deep fryer. They include donuts, onion rings, tempura vegetables, deep-fried Cornish hen, and fish fry.

Food Processor. With the exception of the black bean burgers, I don't think I'd miss my mini food processor that came with my stick blender. If you have limited space, I wouldn't bother with this purchase. If you have hand mobility issues, though, it could come in handy.

Grater. I use a small handheld grater. A box grater is nice, too. Both will do the job just fine.

Knives. I have a nice assortment of knives, and I like to keep them sharp. I own a small v-shaped sharpener that is easy to use. Specifically, I often use a paring knife, a chef's knife, a bread knife, and a potato peeler. I rarely used mid-sized knives, but you may find a mid-sized knife easier to handle than a chef's knife.

Measuring Spoons and Cups. If you can locate them, buy measuring spoons that include a ⅛ teaspoon measure and a ½ tablespoon measure. Any good brand is fine. I also have a Pyrex glass measure for liquids and for melting chocolate in the microwave.

Microwave Oven. I use my microwave to melt chocolate, soften butter, make recipes from my microwave book (*Gluten-Free in Five Minutes*), and to reheat foods.

Mixer. Although I own a KitchenAid stand mixer, I did not use it for a single recipe in this book. It would have been useful for that extra mixing in preparing some icings, but otherwise a hand mixer is fine. I have a Cuisinart hand mixer that is a champ; I have used it for many, many hours in testing recipes for this book.

Plastic Storage Containers. I store flours, sugars, nuts, xanthan gum, and all things baking in plastic containers; some people prefer glass. Whatever you decide to use, just make sure the lids are tight-fitting and seal well.

Pots and Pans. I have simple stainless, triple-clad bottom, pots and pans and think they are the best. The only nonstick pan I own is a small fry pan, which I use for frying eggs. Otherwise, I use a little nonstick spray, and I'm good to go. I do have a large wok. It is triple-clad on the bottom, and I use it extensively to stir-fry.

Rolling Pin. I use a French rolling pin. I find its long narrow shape easy to use. A traditional rolling pin would work just fine. A wine bottle works in a pinch too.

Ruler. This can be helpful in measuring as needed.

Scale. This one is important! I use a Pelouze postage scale, which you can purchase at an office supply store. I value two features, which are not always available on other scales: tare (which resets the scale to zero while a bowl is on the scale) and grams. Measuring flours by weight (grams preferred) is far better than measuring by cup. I do not believe the brand to be as important as these two features.

Small Appliances. A griddle is especially nice when making pancakes. A waffle iron is essential in making waffles. You'll also need a dedicated toaster.

Spoons and Other Utensils. My kitchen would be incomplete without tongs, rubber spatulas, and a whisk. Otherwise, utensils generally found in most kitchens will suffice.

Note: I know that I sometimes sound like an advertisement for Bob's Red Mill flours, and now for Cuisinart appliances. I have no affiliation with either company; I just like their products.

CHAPTER 2

Appetizers

◆

Having something tasty to munch on at a casual gathering or before a meal is such fun! Doing it while hanging out with friends makes it even better. For someone with dietary restrictions, this can also be hard, as so many prepared appetizers may not be safe. These recipes make such gatherings a piece of cake, so to speak.

For a quick treat, hummus and guacamole would be perfect paired with tortilla chips. The sorghum, brown rice, or multigrain crackers would be great on a meat and cheese tray. And the onion rings and plantain fries are, in a word, addictive.

I've also included three types of spring rolls. The Meaty Spring Rolls eat like a meal. The Vegetarian Spring Rolls are pretty traditional. And the Uncooked Spring Rolls are unconventionally good, especially with the dipping sauce!

I also want to point out that the Crab Balls (page 152) make an amazing appetizer!

Black Bean and Fresh Corn Salsa

MAKES 2½ CUPS

❖

It is totally amazing how much corn is on an ear of fresh corn!
If you don't have fresh corn, choose the frozen white shoepeg variety.
This salsa is delicious served with tortilla chips.

1 15.5-ounce can black beans, rinsed and drained

Kernels from 1 fresh ear of corn (or 1 cup frozen corn)

1 small onion, diced

2 tablespoons olive oil

2 tablespoons balsamic vinegar

Small handful fresh parsley, finely chopped (about 1½ tablespoons)

¼ teaspoon cayenne pepper

¼ teaspoon garlic salt

1 teaspoon sugar

1. Place all ingredients into medium bowl. Stir well to combine.

2. Refrigerate for at least an hour, if possible, to allow flavors to blend.

Bonefish Grill–Inspired Mango Salsa

MAKES 2 CUPS

This delicious salsa is sweet with a nice kick from the onion. It is especially tasty served on the Bonefish Grill–Inspired Fish Tacos (page 151).

1 mango, peeled and diced (¼ inch)

1 small onion, diced fine

1½ tablespoons lemon juice

1 tablespoon sugar

1 tablespoon olive oil

¼ teaspoon pepper

1. Place all ingredients into small mixing bowl.
2. Stir well to combine.
3. Refrigerate for one hour, if possible, to allow flavors to blend.

Note: Only 1 cup of salsa is needed for the Bonefish Grill–Inspired Fish Tacos. Save the extra for another time. Try it atop a bed of lettuce and topped with some grilled shrimp. Delicious!

Broiled Mushroom Caps

MAKES 8 MUSHROOM CAPS

◆

This easy appetizer combines the meatiness of mushrooms with the cheesy goodness of quiche. It will be difficult to keep this appetizer exclusively for the gluten-free guest!

8 small white mushrooms

1 egg, beaten

½ ounce shredded cheddar cheese

½ ounce fresh broccoli (a small crown), finely chopped

1. Preheat oven to broil.

2. Brush or wash mushrooms. Remove and discard stems. Place mushroom caps in oven-safe baking dish, upside down.

3. In small bowl, combine egg, cheese, and broccoli. Beat well.

4. Fill mushroom caps with cheese mixture.

5. Broil for approximately 10 minutes until mixture is set, and mushrooms are tender.

Guacamole

MAKES APPROXIMATELY 1 CUP

◆

*The summer of 2012, I enjoyed time at the beach with my children
and feasted on guacamole almost every night because a cousin kept shipping
in avocados from California! Then I came home to duplicate the recipe.
I had epic failures until I realized that I had used the wrong type of avocados.
Choose the smaller, darker Hass avocados! These avocados, when slightly
soft and dark in color, make all the difference in this recipe. I use lemon juice
for a brighter flavor and cumin for an earthy undertone.*

1 avocado, ripe (rather soft when squeezed)

2 teaspoons lemon juice

½ small tomato

1 tablespoon onion, minced

¼ cup cilantro, chopped

⅛ teaspoon salt

⅛ teaspoon cumin (optional)

½ teaspoon hot sauce

1. Remove seed and peel from avocado. Cut into ½-inch cubes. Place into medium-sized bowl.

2. Add lemon juice right away. Stir well.

3. Remove seeds and liquid pulp from tomato. Chop into ¼-inch cubes. Add to bowl.

4. Add remaining ingredients and stir well. Continued stirring will produce a creamy/chunky guacamole. A stick blender may be used to puree the mixture into a smoother guacamole if desired.

Hummus

MAKES 1¼ CUPS

◆

Traditionally, hummus contains sesame tahini, but I have found it's not always easy to locate tahini. Much easier to find is sesame oil. It is delicious and will give us a rich sesame undertone without the shopping frustration! A hint of lemon juice is also used to brighten the flavor of the hummus.

1 15-ounce can chick peas (garbanzo beans)

2 tablespoons retained chick pea liquid

2 tablespoons sesame oil

¼ teaspoon salt

1 teaspoon lemon juice (optional)

1 tablespoon olive oil

1 tablespoon sliced green olives

1. Drain chick peas, retaining liquid. Place chick peas in bowl or into food processor.

2. Add remaining ingredients, except olive oil and sliced olives.

3. Puree until very smooth and creamy. If needed, a bit of retained liquid may be added to achieve a smooth texture.

4. Place pureed hummus into serving dish.

5. Drizzle with olive oil and sliced green olives to garnish.

Hush Puppies (Corn Fritters)

– Brown Rice Flour, Sorghum Flour –
MAKES 15–20 HUSH PUPPIES

✦

These hush puppies have a hint of gumminess if eaten immediately
after frying, so try to let them cool for just a minute for best texture.
The recipe may seem like it calls for a lot of banana pepper rings, but they
are perfect for enhancing the sweet corn flavor of the hush puppies.

2 tablespoons canola oil

$2/3$ cup brown rice flour,
   85 grams

$1/4$ cup sorghum flour,
   35 grams

1 tablespoon sugar

2 egg whites

$1/3$ cup creamed corn

15 to 20 banana pepper slices
   (jarred), chopped

$1/2$ teaspoon baking powder

$1/2$ teaspoon baking soda

$1/2$ teaspoon salt

1 teaspoon xanthan gum

FOR FRYING:

Peanut or canola oil

1. Heat oil, in a saucepan or dedicated deep fryer, to 375°F.

2. Mix flours and oil until well combined.

3. Add remaining ingredients in order, being sure to sprinkle the xanthan gum evenly around to avoid lumps.

4. Beat until well-blended. Then continue beating until dough feels stiff. Then beat just a minute or so longer to develop additional structure.

5. Drop by small rounded teaspoon into hot oil.

6. Fry until hush puppies are lightly browned and cooked through, approximately 1 minute per side. Puppies should be tested for doneness by removing one from the oil and cutting it in half. A well-baked texture should be present completely through the puppies, with no soft middle.

7. Remove from oil and drain on paper towels.

8. Sprinkle lightly with salt.

Appetizers

19

Meaty Spring Rolls

MAKES 6–8 ROLLS

✦

*So often, people are hesitant to try foods that are new or different.
I've combined the classic chicken and mushrooms to make
this appetizer delicious for almost every palate.*

¼ pound ground chicken
(or turkey)

2 medium mushrooms,
finely chopped

1 small onion, minced

1 cup finely chopped bok choy
or grated cabbage (about
4 ounces)

½ teaspoon salt

¼ teaspoon black pepper

6 to 8 spring roll wrappers (rice)

1 egg, beaten

FOR FRYING:

2 tablespoons oil (frying pan)

1 cup oil (deep frying)

1. Heat oil, in a pot or dedicated deep fryer, to 375°F.

2. Stir-fry chicken in oil until no pink remains, just a minute or two.

3. Add remaining ingredients, except wrappers and egg, and sauté until vegetables soften. Set aside to cool.

4. Soften spring roll wrappers very quickly in water, and then drain and set them aside.

5. Place approximately 2 large tablespoons of filling into the center of each rice wrapper. Apply a bit of beaten egg to edge of wrapper. Fold opposite sides over filling, and then roll wrapper into a cylinder shape. With practice, a tightly rolled spring roll will emerge. Repeat for each wrapper and set them aside.

6. Fry until well-browned all over, no more than 5 minutes on each side, or 5 minutes deep-fried.

Note: When making fried spring rolls, it is CRITICAL that you not over-soak the rice wrappers. I did this and couldn't understand why they failed so miserably! Should you find this happens to you, so long as the meat is well cooked, enjoy the "failure" as unfried spring rolls. They're still delicious!

Multigrain Crackers

– Brown Rice Flour, Sorghum Flour, Cornmeal –
MAKES APPROXIMATELY 60 1 1/2-INCH SQUARE CRACKERS

These are light, crispy, whole-grain crackers.

1/2 cup shortening

1 teaspoon apple cider vinegar

1/2 cup brown rice flour,
   65 grams

1/2 cup sorghum flour,
   70 grams

1/2 cup cornmeal, 65 grams

1 tablespoon flax seed meal

1/2 teaspoon baking soda

1/2 teaspoon salt

1 1/2 teaspoons xanthan gum

1/2 cup plain low-fat yogurt

TOPPING:

Salt (flaky sea salt is nice)

1. Preheat the oven to 375°F.

2. Lightly grease a baking sheet.

3. In medium-sized bowl, combine all ingredients, except yogurt. Beat until fine crumbs form. Add yogurt and beat until dough comes together.

4. Pat out dough onto baking sheet as thinly as possible (1/8 inch or less). Use a sharp knife to cut grid pattern across dough to form squares. Use a fork to pierce holes throughout the tops of the crackers. Sprinkle tops with salt.

5. Bake for approximately 10–12 minutes, until tops are lightly browned.

Onion Rings

These onion rings are soaked in buttermilk and coated in a light flour mixture to create a crisp, barely there coating. You will love them, and so will your fellow diners (if you feel like sharing). In You Won't Believe It's Gluten-Free, *you can find batter-dipped onion rings, which are also delicious.*

½ large sweet onion, peeled and sliced into ¼-inch rings

1 cup buttermilk

COATING:

½ cup brown rice flour, 65 grams

¼ cup sorghum flour, 35 grams

¼ teaspoon xanthan gum

¼ teaspoon salt

¼ teaspoon black pepper

⅛ teaspoon baking soda

FOR FRYING:

Peanut or canola oil

1. Heat oil, in a pot or dedicated deep fryer, to 375°F.

2. Mix coating ingredients in large zip-type plastic bag until well combined. Set aside.

3. Place onion rings (slices separated into rings) and buttermilk into a small bowl. Remove ring(s) from buttermilk (do not shake off or try to remove buttermilk) and place them in the coating bag. Shake well and press coating onto the rings to cover well. Carefully place them into hot oil. Do not crowd the rings.

4. Fry until coating is golden brown.

5. Remove onion rings from oil and drain on paper towels. Sprinkle lightly with salt.

Note: To double the yield, double all ingredients except for buttermilk.

Plantain Fries

SERVES 2

✦

*I'm generally not a huge fan of plantains. I am a huge fan of these fries!
You can make these "fries" into chips if you prefer. The plantain should be
light green to yellow in color. Warning, these are addictive.*

1 plantain

¼ teaspoon garlic salt or
   sea salt

FOR FRYING:

Peanut or canola oil

1. Heat oil, in a saucepan or dedicated deep fryer, to 375°F.
2. Peel plantain and cut into strips or slices ⅛ inch thick.
3. Carefully place into oil, and fry until the fries just begin to color, only a minute or two.
4. Remove the fries from the oil and drain them on paper towels. Sprinkle liberally with garlic salt or sea salt.

Snack Crackers

– Brown Rice Flour –
MAKES APPROXIMATELY 60 1½-INCH SQUARE CRACKERS

Here is a brown rice snack cracker. Similar in texture to the sorghum version of Snack Cracker, but lighter in flavor.

½ cup shortening

1 teaspoon apple cider vinegar

1½ cups brown rice flour, 190 grams

½ teaspoon baking soda

½ teaspoon salt

1½ teaspoon xanthan gum

½ cup plain low-fat yogurt

TOPPING:

Salt (flaky sea salt is nice)

1. Preheat the oven to 375°F.

2. Lightly grease a baking sheet.

3. In a medium-sized bowl, combine all ingredients, except yogurt. Beat until fine crumbs form.

4. Add yogurt and beat until dough comes together.

5. Pat out dough onto baking sheet as thinly as possible (⅛ inch or less). Use a sharp knife to cut grid pattern across dough to form squares. Use a fork to pierce holes throughout the tops of the crackers. Sprinkle tops with salt.

6. Bake for approximately 10–12 minutes, until tops are lightly browned.

Snack Crackers

– Sorghum Flour –
MAKES APPROXIMATELY 60 1½-INCH SQUARE CRACKERS

*I consider this cracker much like a Wheat Thin cracker.
I developed this recipe for a sorghum conference in Washington, DC.*

½ cup butter

1 teaspoon apple cider vinegar

1½ cups sorghum flour,
    200 grams

½ teaspoon baking soda

½ teaspoon salt

1½ teaspoons xanthan gum

½ cup plain low-fat yogurt

TOPPING:

Salt (flaky sea salt is nice)

1. Preheat the oven to 375°F.

2. Lightly grease a baking sheet.

3. In a medium-size bowl, combine all ingredients, except yogurt. Beat until fine crumbs form. Add yogurt and beat until dough comes together.

4. Pat out dough onto baking sheet as thinly as possible (⅛ inch or less). Use a sharp knife to cut grid pattern across dough to form squares. Use a fork to pierce holes throughout the tops of the crackers. Sprinkle tops with salt.

5. Bake for approximately 10–12 minutes, until tops are lightly browned.

Tomatoes with Basil and Mozzarella

SERVES 4

This dish is a nice alternative to the traditional tomato and mozzarella salad. It is warm and delicious served alone or with crackers.

8 cherry or grape tomatoes

4 large basil leaves

1 ounce fresh mozzarella cheese

1 tablespoon olive oil

¼ teaspoon salt (approximately)

¼ teaspoon black pepper (approximately)

1. Preheat oven to broil.
2. Cut tomatoes in half and place in oven-safe pan (avoid glass).
3. Cut basil into threads. Sprinkle over tops of tomatoes.
4. Slice cheese into thin slices. Place on tops of tomatoes.
5. Place under broiler until the cheese begins to melt. Do not brown, as basil will become tough.
6. Drizzle tops with olive oil and a sprinkle of salt and pepper.

Uncooked Spring Rolls

MAKES 8 ROLLS

◆

This recipe was a collaborative effort with my daughter, Renee,
who is becoming a fabulous cook. The sauce is her is brain-child. I prefer the
addition of peanut butter to the sauce, giving it more of a traditional Thai flavor,
but even without it, the sauce is quite good! If your rolls are falling apart,
you might want to wrap them in two wrappers instead of one!

1 cup finely chopped bok choy
   or shredded cabbage (about
   4 ounces)

2 tablespoons grated carrots

10 large shrimp, peeled

1 tablespoon sesame oil

1 scallion, finely sliced

2 ounces thin rice noodles

8 spring roll wrappers (rice)

1½ teaspoons soy sauce

½ teaspoon garlic salt

SAUCE:

1½ teaspoons sesame oil

1 tablespoon soy sauce

1½ teaspoons rice vinegar

1½ teaspoons sugar

1½ teaspoons peanut butter
   (optional)

continued on next page

Uncooked Spring Rolls – continued

1. Finely chop the bok choy or shred the cabbage. Place in large bowl.

2. Grate the carrots, and place in the bowl.

3. Stir-fry shrimp in sesame oil until no pink remains, just a minute a minute or two. Remove from heat and set aside. Chop shrimp and add to bowl once they are cooled.

4. Finely slice scallion. Add to bowl.

5. Cook thin rice noodles per package directions. Drain, and add to bowl.

6. Soften spring roll wrappers very quickly in water, and then drain. Set aside.

7. Add soy sauce and garlic salt to bowl. Toss well to combine.

8. Place approximately ¼ cup of filling into center of each rice wrapper. Fold opposite sides over filling, and then roll into a cylinder shape. With practice, a tightly rolled spring roll will emerge. Set aside.

9. Combine all sauce ingredients in a small bowl. Serve on the side for dipping.

Vegetarian Spring Rolls

MAKES 10–12 ROLLS

✦

A tasty, fried version of spring rolls, these appetizers
would also be great for a light lunch or a snack.

1½ cups finely chopped bok choy or grated cabbage (about 6 ounces)

½ cup grated carrots

2 green onions, thinly sliced (tops included)

1 tablespoon soy sauce

1 tablespoon rice wine vinegar

½ teaspoon garlic salt

10 to 12 spring roll wrappers (rice)

1 egg, beaten

FOR FRYING:

2 tablespoons oil (frying pan)

1 cup oil (deep frying)

1. Heat oil, in a saucepan or dedicated deep fryer, to 375°F.

2. Place all ingredients in a large bowl, except wrappers and egg, and mix well. Set aside.

3. Soften spring roll wrappers very quickly in water, and then drain. Set aside.

4. Place approximately 2 large tablespoons of filling into center of each rice wrapper. Apply a bit of beaten egg to the edges. Fold opposite sides over filling, and then roll into a cylinder shape. With practice, a tightly rolled spring roll will emerge. Set aside. Do not worry about any sauce remaining in the bowl.

5. Fry until well-browned all over, no more than 5 minutes on each side, or 5 minutes deep-fried.

Note: Many recipes tell you to stir-fry the vegetables to soften them and blend flavors first. You can certainly do this, but it is not necessary here.

Appetizers

CHAPTER 3

Breakfast

◆

This chapter is full of foods that I could eat every day! (With foods like this, you'll want to eat breakfast for lunch and dinner, too.)

But don't just take my word for it. I've had some pretty diverse testers for my breakfasts.

I had the privilege of preparing breakfast at our local inn, which is owned by Nora Roberts. I made the Ham and Asparagus Breakfast and Fruitinis, which both received rave reviews and only took a few minutes to prepare. I will admit that cooking solo for 16 was a little harder than I first thought.

My boys came home ravenous from college one afternoon. The Sourdough Waffles and Pumpkin Pancakes disappeared very quickly! And the Refrigerator Oatmeal (inspired by my daughter) garnered thank you notes from my houseguests.

But if I had to pick just one extraordinary recipe to make, I'd choose one of the scones. They're just delicious. Or maybe the Coffee Cake Muffins . . . .

Baked French Toast

MAKES 4 SERVINGS

✦

*If you love French toast or bread pudding, here is a collaboration of the two.
It is custardy and delicious. Because canned peaches are so readily available,
they're the perfect fruit to play with in this recipe. Apples and cinnamon
or raisins and nuts would be two other natural choices.*

4 thick slices gluten-free bread

2 peach halves, sliced
(fresh or canned)

¾ cup half and half

2 eggs plus 1 egg yolk

⅓ cup sugar

1 teaspoon vanilla

⅛ teaspoon nutmeg

1. Preheat oven to 350°F.

2. Lightly grease 9-inch square baking dish (or pretty casserole dish).

3. Arrange bread and peach slices in the baking dish. Set aside.

4. Place remaining ingredients in a medium-sized mixing bowl. Mix very well.

5. Pour batter over bread and peaches. Allow to sit for about 5 minutes, so that the bread may absorb the egg mixture.

6. Bake, uncovered, for approximately 20 minutes, until the custard is set, and the top is nicely browned. Serve hot, with syrup, if desired.

Chocolate Cake Donuts

– Brown Rice Flour, Sorghum Flour –
MAKES 12–15 ROUND DONUTS

◆

Unlike many cake donuts, these are quite light!

2 tablespoons canola oil

⅓ cup brown rice flour,
    40 grams

2 tablespoons cocoa

1 tablespoon sorghum flour

3 tablespoons sugar

2 egg whites

¼ cup applesauce

½ teaspoon baking powder

½ teaspoon baking soda

¼ teaspoon salt

1 teaspoon xanthan gum

½ teaspoon vanilla

TOPPING:

½ cup confectioners' or
    plain sugar

FOR FRYING:

Peanut or canola oil

1. Heat oil, in a saucepan or dedicated deep fryer, to 375°F.

2. Mix flours and oil until well combined. Add remaining ingredients in order given, being sure to sprinkle the xanthan gum evenly around to avoid lumps. Beat until well-blended. Then continue beating until dough feels stiff. Then beat just a minute or so longer to develop additional structure.

3. Drop by rounded teaspoon into hot oil.

4. Fry until donuts are dark brown and cooked through, approximately one minute per side. Donuts should be tested for doneness by removing one from the oil and cutting it in half. A well-baked texture should be present throughout the donut, with no soft middle.

5. Remove donuts from oil and drain on paper towels, and then roll in confectioners' sugar or plain sugar.

Coffee Cake

◄◆►

This recipe makes a coffee cake full of cinnamon flavor!
While moist enough to eat alone,
this cake pairs well with a hot cup of tea.

¼ cup butter

¾ cup sorghum flour,
   100 grams

⅓ cup sugar

2 eggs

⅓ cup applesauce

1 tablespoon baking powder

¼ teaspoon baking soda

¼ teaspoon salt

1 teaspoon vanilla

½ teaspoon xanthan gum

TOPPING:

1 tablespoon sorghum flour

1 teaspoon cinnamon

¼ cup brown sugar

3 tablespoons butter

1. Preheat oven to 350°F.

2. Mix flour and butter until well combined.

3. Add remaining ingredients. Beat well for about 1 minute. Batter will thicken nicely.

4. Pour into lightly greased 9-inch round (or square) baking pan.

5. Combine topping ingredients into a crumble. Sprinkle over top of batter.

6. Bake 20–25 minutes, until a toothpick inserted in the middle tests clean, and the cake is lightly browned on top.

You Still Won't Believe It's Gluten-Free

Coffee Cake Muffins

– Brown Rice Flour –
MAKES 9 MUFFINS

✦

*Cinnamon, vanilla, and nuts are key ingredients in these
wonderful coffee cake muffins. I love pairing pecans and vanilla,
but use whatever nuts you like.*

¼ cup butter

¾ cup brown rice flour,
   95 grams

⅓ cup sugar

2 eggs

⅓ cup applesauce

1 tablespoon baking powder

¼ teaspoon baking soda

¼ teaspoon salt

1 teaspoon vanilla

½ teaspoon xanthan gum

TOPPING:

1 tablespoon brown rice flour

1 teaspoon cinnamon

¼ cup finely chopped pecans

¼ cup brown sugar

3 tablespoons butter

1. Preheat oven to 350°F.
2. Mix flour and butter until well combined.
3. Add remaining ingredients. Beat well for about 1 minute. Batter will thicken nicely.
4. Pour into 9 lined muffin cups. I like to use foil muffin liners with the muffin tin.
5. Combine topping ingredients into a crumble. Sprinkle over top of batter.
6. Bake 15–20 minutes, until a toothpick inserted in the middle of one muffin tests clean, and muffins are lightly browned on top.

Fruitinis

MAKES 4 SERVINGS.

◆

*It's hardly fair to call this a recipe, but it merits inclusion in this book.
The difference between a bowl of fruit at breakfast and a
"hmm . . . what is awesomely different here?" is quite substantial.
People will wonder how you made the fruit taste so very good!*

1 cup blueberries

1 pint strawberries

1 cup raspberries or
blackberries

¼ cup sugar

½ teaspoon vanilla

1. Wash fruit well.

2. Slice strawberries and place all fruit
in large bowl.

3. Gently toss with sugar and vanilla.

4. Spoon into goblets and chill until
serving.

Fruitini Parfaits: For a lovely parfait,
layer prepared fruit with vanilla yogurt
and gluten-free granola. This presentation received wonderful reviews at the
local inn.

Grits for Breakfast

MAKES 2 CUPS

*Are you craving hot cereal for breakfast that is hearty like oatmeal,
but your local market doesn't carry a gluten-free variety? Here's the answer.
This version tastes like a hot cinnamon roll (with raisins).*

½ cup grits

2 cups cold water

2 tablespoons sugar

½ teaspoon vanilla

½ teaspoon cinnamon

½ cup raisins

Scant ⅛ teaspoon salt

2 tablespoons butter

1. In a medium saucepan, cover grits with cold water according to package directions. Add remaining ingredients, except butter.

2. Slowly bring to a boil. Simmer until quite thick, approximately 5 minutes.

3. Stir in butter. Serve hot.

Note: A freshly chopped apple or nuts would make great alternatives to raisins!

Ham and Asparagus Skillet Breakfast

SERVES 1 OR 2

✦

Classic flavors combine for a delicious breakfast.
Eggs have never tasted so good!

1 tablespoon canola oil

3 to 4 ounces country ham, diced (¼ inch)

4 ounces fresh asparagus, cut into 1-inch slices

2 eggs

Pepper to garnish

1. Place oil in a small skillet. Add diced ham and cook over medium-high heat until cooked through, approximately 5 minutes.

2. Add asparagus and cook until lightly seared, approximately 1 minute.

3. Push ham and asparagus to the sides of the pan, leaving a space in the middle. Crack both eggs into the center.

4. Turn heat to low. Cover and cook until whites are set, approximately 3 to 4 minutes.

5. Once eggs are cooked, sprinkle pepper over the eggs. Serve from skillet or slide onto a serving plate.

6. Serve hot.

Light Cake Donuts

– Brown Rice Flour, Sorghum Flour –
MAKES 12–15 ROUND DONUTS

◆

If you're craving a yeast-type donut, you'll need to pull the recipe from my first book, The Gluten-Free Kitchen. *In this book, we are focusing on healthier flours, which will produce a light cake donut.*

2 tablespoons canola oil

½ cup brown rice flour, 40 grams

2 tablespoons sorghum flour

2 tablespoons sugar

2 egg whites

¼ cup applesauce

½ teaspoon baking powder

½ teaspoon baking soda

¼ teaspoon salt

1 teaspoon xanthan gum

1 teaspoon apple cider vinegar

¼ teaspoon vanilla

TOPPING:

½ cup confectioners' or plain sugar

FOR FRYING:

Peanut or canola oil

1. Heat oil, in a saucepan or dedicated deep fryer, to 375°F.

2. Mix flours and oil until well combined. Add remaining ingredients in order given, being sure to sprinkle the xanthan gum around evenly to avoid lumps. Beat until well-blended. Then continue beating until dough feels stiff. Then beat just a minute or so longer to develop additional structure.

3. Drop by rounded teaspoon into hot oil.

4. Fry until donuts are lightly browned and cooked through, approximately 1 minute per side. Donuts should be tested for doneness by removing one from the oil and cutting it in half. A well-baked texture should be present completely through the donut, with no soft middle.

5. Remove from oil and drain on paper towels, and then roll in confectioners' sugar or plain sugar.

My Favorite Sourdough Pancakes

– Brown Rice Flour, Sorghum Flour –
MAKES 6–7 4-INCH PANCAKES

Here are some absolutely delicious pancakes.
I like the added bit of vanilla, but it is not necessary!

2 eggs

½ cup brown rice flour,
   65 grams

¼ cup sorghum flour,
   35 grams

1 tablespoon baking powder

¼ cup canola oil

¼ teaspoon salt

2 tablespoons sugar

½ teaspoon xanthan gum

½ cup Sourdough Starter
   (page 59)

½ teaspoon vanilla

⅓ cup milk

1. Heat pan or griddle to medium heat. A drop of water should "dance" on the surface.

2. Place all ingredients in a medium-sized mixing bowl. (I like to add the milk last, as the batter will thicken upon sitting.) Mix well. Batter will become quite thick.

3. Pour batter to desired size. Spread with a spoon if necessary. Cook until small bubbles appear on the surface, and pancakes are lightly browned. Flip and continue cooking until cakes are lightly browned on both sides.

Pancakes

– Brown Rice Flour –
MAKES 6–7 4-INCH PANCAKES

These pancakes are light,
buttery, and delicious.

2 eggs

¾ cup brown rice flour,
95 grams

1 tablespoon baking powder

¼ cup butter, melted

¼ teaspoon salt

2 tablespoons sugar

½ teaspoon xanthan gum

¾ cup milk

1. Heat pan or griddle to medium heat. A drop of water should "dance" on the surface.

2. Place all ingredients in a medium-sized mixing bowl. (I like to add the milk last, as the batter will thicken upon sitting.) Mix well. Batter will become quite thick.

3. Pour batter to desired size. Spread with a spoon if necessary. Cook until small bubbles appear on the surface, and pancakes are lightly browned. Flip and continue cooking until cakes are lightly browned on both sides.

Pancakes

– Sorghum Flour –
MAKES 6–7 4-INCH PANCAKES

◆◆

Sorghum flour works well in pancakes.
If you like a "wheaty" flavor, you will like these.

2 eggs

¾ cup sorghum flour,
   100 grams

1 tablespoon baking powder

¼ cup canola oil

¼ teaspoon salt

1½ tablespoons sugar

½ teaspoon xanthan gum

½ teaspoon vanilla

¾ cup milk

1. Heat pan or griddle to medium heat. A drop of water should "dance" on the surface.

2. Place all ingredients in a medium-sized mixing bowl. (I like to add the milk last, as the batter will thicken upon sitting.) Mix well. Batter will become quite thick.

3. Pour batter to desired size. Spread with a spoon if necessary. Cook until small bubbles appear on the surface, and pancakes are lightly browned. Flip and continue cooking until cakes are lightly browned on both sides.

Pasta Frittata

SERVES 2

*One of my favorite quick breakfasts is to make eggs with pasta.
Traditional . . . no. Delicious . . . yes. Delicate, yet very flavorful,
it's a perfect way to use any leftover pasta! This dish is best prepared
with a nonstick pan. I like to add a sprinkling of freshly ground sea salt just
before serving, but a sprinkling of Parmesan cheese would also be nice.*

2 tablespoons oil
(canola or olive)

¾ cup cooked pasta, any kind

4 eggs

1 tablespoon water

8 spears of asparagus or 1 cup
broccoli crowns, chopped

¼ cup fresh bell peppers
(red or yellow are especially
pretty), chopped

¼ cup onion, chopped

2 smallish mushrooms, chopped

1½ teaspoons rosemary (dried)

¼ teaspoon salt

⅛ teaspoon black pepper

1 tablespoon water

1. Place eggs, salt, pepper, water, and rosemary in a bowl. Beat well. Set aside.

2. In large skillet or frying pan, place oil and heat to medium heat.

3. Sauté mushrooms until tender. Add in other veggies and cook until tender-crisp.

4. Arrange veggies in a pretty pattern if desired.

5. Add pasta and pour egg mixture over top. Reduce heat to low and cover.

6. Cook until eggs are done, less than 4 minutes. When eggs are "set," slide onto serving plate. Add a final sprinkle of freshly ground sea salt or Parmesan cheese.

Note: Try this dish with almost any extra pasta, even clear rice noodles.

Breakfast

43

Pumpkin Pancakes

– Brown Rice Flour –
MAKES 8 4-INCH PANCAKES

I have to admit that when I was developing this recipe (at the prompting of my daughter—a bona-fide pumpkin lover), I was hesitant. But these pancakes are light and spicy, and their flavor really comes to life the moment syrup is poured over them! They are a lovely change of pace.

2 eggs

½ cup brown rice flour,
   65 grams

¼ cup sorghum flour,
   35 grams

1 tablespoon baking powder

¼ cup canola oil

¼ teaspoon salt

2 tablespoons sugar

½ teaspoon xanthan gum

½ cup pumpkin

¾ cup milk

½ teaspoon cinnamon

⅛ teaspoon nutmeg

1. Heat pan or griddle to medium heat. A drop of water should "dance" on the surface.

2. Place all ingredients in a medium-sized mixing bowl. (I like to add the milk last, as the batter will thicken upon sitting.) Mix well. Batter will become quite thick.

3. Pour batter to desired size. Spread with a spoon if necessary. Cook until small bubbles appear on the surface, and pancakes are lightly browned. Flip and continue cooking until cakes are lightly browned on both sides.

Refrigerator Oatmeal

MAKES 1 ½ CUPS. SERVES 2

✦

*This recipe was inspired by my daughter. It's one part oats,
one part milk, one part applesauce, plus imagination! Pecans and
cranberries were my choice, but let your imagination run wild!*

½ cup oats (thinner milled is better)

½ cup milk (almond milk is especially nice)

½ cup applesauce (or your favorite sweetened yogurt)

¼ cup dried cranberries

¼ cup chopped pecans

¼ teaspoon vanilla

¼ teaspoon cinnamon

1. Combine all ingredients in a medium-sized bowl. Mix well.

2. Pour into individual serving dishes if desired.

3. Cover tightly and place in the refrigerator overnight. Serve hot or cold.

Scones

– Brown Rice Flour –
MAKES 12 SMALL SCONES

✦

The sorghum version of my scones is so yummy that I had to make these with brown rice flour as well. I've used cherries and chocolate chips in this version. Like most biscuits and scones, they are better the fresher they are!

½ cup butter

1 cup brown rice flour, 125 grams

1¼ teaspoons xanthan gum

1 tablespoon baking powder

½ teaspoon baking soda

2 tablespoons sugar

¼ teaspoon salt

⅓ cup dried cherries, roughly chopped

¼ cup chocolate chips

½ cup half and half

1 egg

1 teaspoon apple cider vinegar

TOPS:

1 tablespoon butter, melted (optional)

GLAZE:

3 tablespoons confectioners' sugar

Several drops vanilla

1 teaspoon half and half

1. Preheat oven to 375°F.

2. In a medium-sized bowl, blend all ingredients, except dried cherries, chips, half and half, egg, and vinegar to fine crumb.

3. Add dried cherries, chips, milk, and vinegar. Mix well until combined into soft, sticky dough. It will be quite fragile.

4. Pat dough on a greased baking sheet into a rectangle ½ inch thick.

5. Cut into 12 squares, and use the side of the knife to separate them slightly.

6. Brush tops with melted butter, if using.

7. Bake for 15–20 minutes, until biscuits begin to brown.

8. Combine glaze ingredients and drizzle over scones.

Scones

– Sorghum Flour –
MAKES 12 SMALL SCONES

Scones are the "rich" cousin to biscuits. A little cream (or half and half)
plus an egg, a little extra sugar, a little fruit, and there you have it. I have used
dried cranberries in this recipe, but dried cherries, raisins, or even nuts
would be great options. These are not good; they are delicious!

½ cup butter

1 cup sorghum flour, 135 grams

1¼ teaspoons xanthan gum

1 tablespoon baking powder

½ teaspoon baking soda

2½ tablespoons sugar

¼ teaspoon salt

½ cup dried cranberries,
  roughly chopped

½ cup half and half

1 egg

1 teaspoon apple cider vinegar

TOPS:

1 tablespoon butter, melted
  (optional)

GLAZE:

3 tablespoons confectioners'
  sugar

Several drops vanilla

1 teaspoon half and half

1. Preheat oven to 375°F.

2. In a medium-sized bowl, blend all ingredients, except cranberries, milk, egg, and vinegar to fine crumb.

3. Add cranberries, milk, and vinegar. Mix well until combined into soft, sticky dough. It will be quite fragile.

4. Pat dough onto greased baking sheet into a rectangle ½ inch thick.

5. Cut into 12 squares and use the side of the knife to separate them slightly.

6. Brush with melted butter, if using.

7. Bake for 15–20 minutes, until scones begin to brown.

8. Combine glaze ingredients and drizzle over scones.

Sourdough Waffles

– Brown Rice Flour –
MAKES 6 4-INCH WAFFLES

I tested these waffles the day before my children came home on spring break. I put the extras in the refrigerator, thinking they might enjoy having breakfast with me. The waffles didn't last that long; they were the first item removed and devoured—simply reheated in the toaster.

3 egg whites

3 egg yolks

¾ cup brown rice flour, 95 grams

1 tablespoon baking powder

¼ cup canola oil

¼ teaspoon salt

2 tablespoons sugar

½ cup Sourdough Starter (page 59)

¼ cup milk

¾ teaspoon xanthan gum

1. Preheat the waffle iron.

2. Beat egg whites to stiff peaks. Set aside.

3. Place remaining ingredients in a medium-sized mixing bowl. Mix well, but avoid excess beating.

4. Fold in egg whites.

5. Place full ⅓ to ½ cup batter into waffle iron (per small square). Cook to desired level of browning, about 1½ to 2 minutes.

Waffles

◆

These waffles are light with a hint of sweetness.
They are really a very nice waffle.

3 egg whites

3 egg yolks

1 cup sorghum flour,
   135 grams

1 tablespoon plus 1 teaspoon
   baking powder

⅓ cup canola oil

¼ teaspoon salt

2 tablespoons sugar

¾ cup milk

¾ teaspoon xanthan gum

½ teaspoon vanilla

1. Preheat waffle iron.

2. Beat egg whites to stiff peaks.
   Set aside.

3. Place remaining ingredients in
   a medium-sized mixing bowl.
   Mix well.

4. Fold in egg whites.

5. Place full ⅓ cup of batter into
   waffle iron (per small square).
   Cook to desired level of browning,
   about 1½ to 2 minutes.

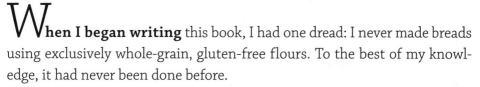

CHAPTER 4

Breads—Loaves

When I began writing this book, I had one dread: I never made breads using exclusively whole-grain, gluten-free flours. To the best of my knowledge, it had never been done before.

Once again, I found myself at a food-science crossroad. Would everything I learned in making cakes, cookies, and muffins with whole-grain flours apply to making great breads? With a leap of faith and encouragement from my food scientist friend, Sara, I jumped into this chapter.

I am pleased to say, these are the best gluten-free loaves of bread I have ever made. The Everyday Soft Loaves are very light and, well, very soft. The Yeast-Free "Mighty" Bread is a whole-grain bread-lover's new favorite. The Artisan Bread is a good, medium-dense textured bread that could be used for anything.

For those of you who have had yeast-breads made with flour blends, you may have noticed a certain aftertaste. The great news is that that aftertaste does not exist in these breads. The flavor is very, very good.

Bread theory enables us to achieve really great textures. These recipes use three approaches at one time to achieve great texture: First, an egg white foam adds lift and structure; second, a chemical raising agent (baking powder) lifts and adds rise to the loaf; and finally, yeast adds a final push of lift and flavor.

I'm seeing a lot of sandwiches in someone's future.

Tips to make yeast breads rise

When making yeast breads, it is really nice to get that extra push in rise by allowing the dough some time in a warm place. I create a warm, moist environment in my microwave. It's easy.

Place one cup of water in the microwave. I like to use a pyrex measuring cup. Cook on high for three minutes. Open the microwave. Carefully move the cup of boiling water to a corner. Place dough (in pan) in the microwave and close the door. The goal is to keep the inside of the microwave pleasantly warm and moist, so move fast!

After the dough achieves a nice rise, you'll be ready to bake it in the oven.

The temperature of the wet ingredients also affects how fast dough rises. Eggs can be brought to room temperature in just a few minutes by placing them in a bowl of warm water. Liquids can be warmed before use—but don't make them hot.

All of these actions will speed up your rise time for yeast-containing breads. If you don't utilize these methods, just know that it will take a little (or a lot) longer for your bread to rise.

Artisan Bread

– White Rice Flour –
MAKES 1 LOAF. SERVES 9

*Here is a strong, stable loaf of plain white bread.
It has a nice chew and would satisfy non-gluten-free bread eaters, too.*

2 tablespoons canola oil

1½ cups white rice flour,
   230 grams

1 tablespoon brown sugar

3 egg whites, room temperature

½ cup applesauce

2 teaspoons baking powder

¼ teaspoon baking soda

½ teaspoon salt

2½ teaspoons xanthan gum

1 tablespoon (or one packet)
   yeast, dissolved in
   2 tablespoons water

TOPPING:

1 teaspoon white rice flour

1. Preheat oven to 350°F.
2. Mix flour and oil until well combined.
3. Add remaining ingredients in order given, being sure to sprinkle the xanthan gum around evenly to avoid lumps. Beat until well blended. Then continue beating until dough feels stiff. Then beat another minute or so to develop additional structure.
4. Place dough in the center of a lightly greased baking sheet. Shape into oval or round loaf as desired. Smooth with moistened (or greased) fingertips. Sprinkle flour over the top.
5. With a very sharp knife, cut several slits on the top of the loaf.
6. Let rise for about 30–40 minutes in a warm spot. Dough should double in size.
7. Bake approximately 20–25 minutes, until toothpick inserted in the middle tests clean, and the loaf is lightly browned on top.

Everyday Soft Loaf

– Brown Rice Flour –
MAKES 1 LOAF. SERVES 9

I received a wonderful hint from a certain food-scientist friend of mine:
Use honey with brown rice flour! This loaf of bread rocks!

2 tablespoons canola oil

1¼ cups brown rice flour,
   155 grams

2 tablespoons honey

4 egg whites, room temperature

½ cup warm water

2 teaspoons baking powder

¼ teaspoon baking soda

½ teaspoon salt

1½ teaspoons xanthan gum

1 tablespoon (or one packet)
   yeast, dissolved in
   2 tablespoons water

1. Preheat oven to 350°F.

2. Mix flour and oil until well combined.

3. Add remaining ingredients in the order given, being sure to sprinkle the xanthan gum around evenly to avoid lumps. Beat until well blended. Then continue beating until dough feels stiff.

4. Pour into a greased loaf pan.

5. Let dough rise for about 45 minutes in a warm spot. Bread should double in size. The top of the bread should be ¼ inch from the top of the pan.

6. Bake approximately 25 minutes, until a toothpick inserted in the middle tests clean, and the loaf is lightly browned on top.

Everyday Soft Loaf

– Brown Rice Flour, Sorghum Flour –
MAKES 1 LOAF. SERVES 9

✦

*While almost all of the other recipes in this book use just one flour,
this combination of brown rice flour with a hint of sorghum flour makes a pretty
amazing loaf of bread, hugely reminiscent of traditional wheat-based bread.*

2 tablespoons canola oil

1 cup brown rice flour,
  125 grams

¼ cup sorghum flour,
  35 grams

1 tablespoon sugar

4 egg whites, room temperature

½ cup warm water

2 teaspoons baking powder

¼ teaspoon baking soda

½ teaspoon salt

1½ teaspoons xanthan gum

1 tablespoon (or one packet)
  yeast, dissolved in
  2 tablespoons water

1. Preheat oven to 350°F.

2. Mix flours and oil until well combined.

3. Add remaining ingredients in the order given, being sure to sprinkle the xanthan gum around evenly to avoid lumps. Beat until well blended. Then continue beating until dough feels stiff.

4. Pour into a greased loaf pan.

5. Let dough rise for about 45 minutes in a warm spot. Bread should double in size. The top of the bread should be ¼ inch from the top of the pan.

6. Bake approximately 25 minutes, until a toothpick inserted in the middle tests clean, and the loaf is lightly browned on top.

Breads—Loaves

Everyday Soft Loaf

– Sorghum Flour –
MAKES 1 LOAF. SERVES 9

*I decided to use as few ingredients as possible in making
this loaf of bread. It will take a while to rise, but it is quite easy.
It will stay moist for days. No toasting is required.*

2 tablespoons canola oil

1¼ cups sorghum flour,
    135 grams

1 tablespoon sugar

4 egg whites, room temperature

½ cup warm water

2 teaspoons baking powder

¼ teaspoon baking soda

½ teaspoon salt

1½ teaspoons xanthan gum

1 tablespoon (or one packet)
    yeast, dissolved in
    2 tablespoons water

1. Preheat oven to 350°F.

2. Mix flour and oil until well combined.

3. Add remaining ingredients in the order given, being sure to sprinkle the xanthan gum around evenly to avoid lumps. Beat until well blended. Then continue beating until dough feels stiff.

4. Pour into a greased loaf pan.

5. Let dough rise for about 45 minutes in a warm spot. Bread should double in size. The top of the bread should be ¼ inch from the top of the pan.

6. Bake approximately 25 minutes, until a toothpick inserted in the middle tests clean, and the loaf is lightly browned on top.

My Favorite Yeast-Free Bread

– Brown Rice Flour, Sorghum Flour –
MAKES 1 LOAF. SERVES 9

In many commercially available breads, a "base" flour is often combined with just a bit of another flour. I've used that theory quite successfully in this bread. It is my favorite go-to loaf!

2 tablespoons canola oil

¾ cup brown rice flour, 95 grams

¼ cup sorghum flour, 35 grams

2 teaspoons honey

3 egg whites, room temperature

½ cup applesauce

1 teaspoon baking powder

1 teaspoon baking soda

½ teaspoon salt

2 teaspoons xanthan gum

1 tablespoon apple cider vinegar

1. Preheat oven to 375°F.

2. Mix flours and oil until well combined.

3. Add remaining ingredients in the order given, being sure to sprinkle the xanthan gum around evenly to avoid lumps. Beat until well blended. Then continue beating until the dough feels stiff. Then beat just a minute or so longer to develop additional structure.

4. Dump dough onto a lightly greased baking sheet and shape into a pretty oval or round loaf using moist fingertips.

5. Cut a few slits across the top of the loaf for expansion during baking.

6. Bake for 20–25 minutes, until a toothpick inserted in the middle tests clean, and the loaf is lightly browned on top. Avoid over-baking, as the bottom of the loaf will brown quicker than the top of the loaf.

Breads—Loaves

Sourdough Bread

– Brown Rice Flour –
MAKES 1 LOAF. SERVES 9

This bread has a nice sourdough undertone. If you like more kick to the sourdough taste, just allow the starter to develop for a longer period of time: 24 hours makes for quite a nice starter. The crust on this bread is especially nice.

2 tablespoons canola oil

1½ cups brown rice flour, 190 grams

2 teaspoons sugar

3 egg whites, room temperature

¼ cup applesauce

½ cup Sourdough Starter (page 59)

2 teaspoons baking powder

¼ teaspoon baking soda

½ teaspoon salt

2½ teaspoons xanthan gum

1. Preheat oven to 350°F.

2. Mix flour and oil until well combined.

3. Add remaining ingredients in the order given, being sure to sprinkle the xanthan gum around evenly to avoid lumps. Beat until well blended. Then continue beating until dough feels stiff. Then beat another minute or so to develop additional structure.

4. Place dough in the center of a lightly greased baking sheet. Shape into an oval or round loaf as desired. Smooth with moistened (or greased) fingertips.

5. With a very sharp knife, cut several slits on the top of the loaf.

6. Let dough rise for about 30–40 minutes in a warm spot. Loaf should double in size.

7. Bake approximately 20–25 minutes, until a toothpick inserted in the middle tests clean, and the loaf is lightly browned on top.

Sourdough Starter

– Brown Rice Flour –

Having a bread starter ready in the refrigerator makes bread, pancakes, waffles, rolls, pizza crust—just about everything—tasty! Just add ½ cup starter to almost any recipe. This starter quickly becomes quite sour. If you are keeping it for several days (or even longer), be sure to feed it a little flour (and water) at least every other day so that the yeast remains active.

1 tablespoon (or 1 packet) yeast

½ cup warm water

½ cup brown rice flour

1 teaspoon sugar

1. Mix all ingredients well in a large bowl.

2. Set out at room temperature for an hour, and stir every 15 minutes or so. Store it overnight in the refrigerator.

3. Stir well before using.

White Bread

– White Rice Flour –
MAKES 1 LOAF. SERVES 9

This is a traditional plain, ordinary loaf of white bread, baked in a 4x8-inch loaf pan. Yeast gives this loaf extra volume, while the vinegar adds a bit of yeasty taste. For best results, you'll want to bring the egg whites and yogurt to room temperature.

2 tablespoons canola oil

¾ cup white rice flour, 115 grams

1 tablespoon sugar

4 egg whites, room temperature

½ cup plain low-fat yogurt

2 teaspoons baking powder

¼ teaspoon baking soda

½ teaspoon salt

1½ teaspoons xanthan gum

1 tablespoon (or one packet) yeast, dissolved in 1 tablespoon water

1. Preheat oven to 350°F.

2. Mix flour and oil until well combined.

3. Add remaining ingredients in the order given, being sure to sprinkle the xanthan gum around evenly to avoid lumps. Beat until well blended. Then continue beating until the dough feels stiff.

4. Pour into a greased loaf pan.

5. Let dough rise for about 45 minutes in a warm spot. Bread should double in size. The top of the bread should be ¼ inch from the top of the pan.

6. Bake approximately 25 minutes, until a toothpick inserted in the middle tests clean, and the loaf is lightly browned on top.

Yeast-Free "Mighty" Bread

– Brown Rice Flour –
MAKES 1 LOAF. SERVES 9

Here's a really tasty, grain-intense bread. By using Bob's Red Mill Mighty Tasty Hot Cereal, you don't need to buy a huge variety of flours. And, the hot cereal is also very tasty, too.

2 tablespoons canola oil

¾ cup brown rice flour, 95 grams

½ cup Bob's Red Mill Mighty Tasty Hot Cereal

2 teaspoons honey

3 egg whites, room temperature

½ cup applesauce

1 teaspoon baking powder

1 teaspoon baking soda

½ teaspoon salt

2 teaspoons xanthan gum

1 tablespoon apple cider vinegar

1. Preheat oven to 375°F.

2. Mix flour, cereal, and oil until well combined.

3. Add remaining ingredients in the order given, being sure to sprinkle the xanthan gum around evenly to avoid lumps. Beat until well-blended. Then continue beating until dough feels stiff. Then beat just a minute or so longer to develop additional structure.

4. Dump dough onto a lightly greased baking sheet and shape into a pretty oval or round loaf using moist fingertips. Cut a few slits across the top of the loaf for expansion during baking.

5. Bake for 20–25 minutes, until a toothpick inserted in the middle tests clean, and the loaf is lightly browned on top. Avoid over-baking as the bottom of the loaf will brown quicker than the top of the loaf.

Yeast-Free Brown Rice and Corn Loaf

– Brown Rice Flour, Cornmeal –
MAKES 1 LOAF. SERVES 9

This is a pretty little loaf of bread that I make free-form on a baking sheet.

2 tablespoons canola oil

¾ cup brown rice flour,
    95 grams

¼ cup cornmeal, 30 grams

1½ teaspoons sugar

3 egg whites, room temperature

½ cup applesauce

1 teaspoon baking powder

1 teaspoon baking soda

½ teaspoon salt

2 teaspoons xanthan gum

1 tablespoon apple cider
    vinegar

1. Preheat oven to 375°F.

2. Mix flour, cornmeal, and oil until well combined.

3. Add remaining ingredients in the order given, being sure to sprinkle the xanthan gum around evenly to avoid lumps. Beat until well-blended. Then continue beating until dough feels stiff. Then beat just a minute or so longer to develop additional structure.

4. Dump dough onto a lightly greased baking sheet, and shape into a pretty oval or round loaf using moist fingertips. Cut a few slits across the top of the loaf for expansion during baking.

5. Bake for 20–25 minutes, until a toothpick inserted in the middle tests clean, and the loaf is lightly browned on top. Avoid over-baking as the bottom of the loaf will brown quicker than the top of the loaf.

Yeast-Free Oat Flake Bread

– Brown Rice Flour, Sorghum Flour –
MAKES 1 LOAF. SERVES 9

✦

Gluten-free oats can be dry and a bit difficult to use in bread recipes. In order to use them here, you can either give them a quick chop in a food processor or combine them with just a little water and microwave for 20 seconds to soften.

2 tablespoons canola oil

¾ cup brown rice flour, 95 grams

¼ cup sorghum flour, 35 grams

½ cup rolled oats, lightly processed in food processor

1 tablespoon honey

3 egg whites, room temperature

½ cup applesauce

1 teaspoon baking powder

1 teaspoon baking soda

½ teaspoon salt

2 teaspoons xanthan gum

1 tablespoon apple cider vinegar

1. Preheat oven to 375°F.
2. Mix flours and oil until well combined.
3. Add remaining ingredients in the order given, being sure to sprinkle the xanthan gum around evenly to avoid lumps. Beat until well-blended. Then continue beating until dough feels stiff. Then beat just a minute or so longer to develop additional structure.
4. Dump dough onto a lightly greased baking sheet, and shape into a pretty oval or round loaf using moist fingertips. Cut a few slits across the top of the loaf for expansion during baking.
5. Bake for 20–25 minutes, until a toothpick inserted in the middle tests clean, and the loaf is lightly browned on top. Avoid over-baking as the bottom of the loaf will brown quicker than the top of the loaf.

Yeast-Free Sweet Bread with Cinnamon and Raisins

– Brown Rice Flour –
MAKES 1 LOAF. SERVES 9

This bread has great structure and will hold up to whatever you want to put on it (and it tastes great all by itself, too). By folding the cinnamon and raisins into the dough, you end up with a rustic-looking loaf.

2 tablespoons canola oil

1 cup brown rice flour, 125 grams

2 tablespoons honey

3 egg whites, room temperature

½ cup applesauce

1 teaspoon baking powder

1 teaspoon baking soda

½ teaspoon salt

2 teaspoons xanthan gum

1 tablespoon apple cider vinegar

1 teaspoon cinnamon

½ cup raisins

1. Preheat oven to 375°F.
2. Mix flour and oil until well combined.
3. Add remaining ingredients in order, being sure to sprinkle the xanthan gum around evenly to avoid lumps. Beat until well-blended. Then continue beating until dough feels stiff. Then beat just a minute or so longer to develop additional structure.
4. Sprinkle raisins and cinnamon over the dough, and gently fold them into the dough.
5. Dump dough onto a lightly greased baking sheet, and shape into a pretty oval or round loaf using moist fingertips. Cut a few slits across the top of the loaf for expansion during baking.
6. Bake for 20–25 minutes, until a toothpick inserted in the middle tests clean, and the loaf is lightly browned on top. Avoid over-baking, as the bottom of loaf will brown quicker than the top of the loaf.

CHAPTER 5

Breads—Rolls, Flatbread, Pizza Crusts, etc.

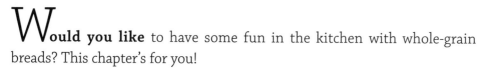

Would **you like** to have some fun in the kitchen with whole-grain breads? This chapter's for you!

My Naan, an Indian flatbread, is crisp on the base and light and airy on the top. It is slightly lighter in texture than traditional naan. Also, you don't need a traditional tandoor oven to make these in your own kitchen.

If you're a pizza lover, it's time to make pizza! In fact, these are some of the best gluten-free crusts I've ever eaten.

Another fun change of pace is My Favorite Flatbread. It is pliable and doesn't fall apart. It would be perfect for fish tacos or fajitas.

Once you try one recipe in this chapter, I think you'll try many of them. They are that good.

Cinnamon Rolls

– Brown Rice Flour –
MAKES 7–8 ROLLS

The original cinnamon rolls in my first book, The Gluten-Free Kitchen *were one of my claims to fame. I decided to see if I could improve on the recipe, and it was truly worth the effort! These are best enjoyed on the day you make them.*

DOUGH:

2 tablespoons canola oil

1½ cups brown rice flour, 190 grams

2 tablespoon sugar

1 egg plus 2 egg whites, room temperature

½ cup applesauce

2 teaspoons baking powder

¼ teaspoon baking soda

½ teaspoon salt

2 teaspoons xanthan gum

1 tablespoon (or one packet) yeast, dissolved in 2 tablespoons water

½ teaspoon vanilla

FILLING:

1 cup brown sugar

1¼ teaspoons cinnamon

TOPPING (OR BOTTOM):

½ cup chopped pecans

¼ cup brown sugar

2 tablespoons butter, melted

1. Preheat oven to 375°F.

2. Combine filling ingredients. Set aside.

3. Combine ingredients for topping (which starts at the bottom of the pan) in a small bowl. Place in the bottom of a lightly greased 8-inch round cake pan. Set aside.

4. Mix flour and oil until well combined. Add remaining ingredients in the order given, being sure to sprinkle the xanthan gum around evenly to avoid lumps. Beat until well-blended. Then continue beating until dough feels stiff.

5. On a greased countertop (or greased waxed paper or foil), pat dough into a rectangle about 12 inches x 12 inches and ¼-inch thick.

6. Combine brown sugar and cinnamon. Sprinkle over top of dough. Gently roll dough into a log. Cut into 1½-inch wide slices (7 or 8 slices) and place them in the baking pan on top of the nut/sugar mixture.

7. Let rise for about 30–40 minutes in a warm spot. Rolls should double in size.

8. Bake approximately 15–20 minutes, until a toothpick inserted in the middle of one tests clean, and the rolls are lightly browned on top.

9. Carefully cover rolls with a serving plate and invert for serving.

Dinner Rolls

– Brown Rice Flour –
SERVES 9

These are soft, tender, buttery dinner rolls.

3 tablespoons butter, melted

¾ cup brown rice flour,
   95 grams

1 tablespoon sugar

3 egg whites, room temperature

½ cup warm milk

2 teaspoons baking powder

¼ teaspoon baking soda

½ teaspoon salt

1½ teaspoons xanthan gum

1 tablespoon (or one packet)
   yeast, dissolved in
   2 tablespoons water

1. Preheat oven to 350°F.

2. Mix flour and butter until well combined. Add remaining ingredients in the order given, being sure to sprinkle the xanthan gum around evenly to avoid lumps. Beat until well-blended. Then continue beating until dough feels stiff.

3. With an ice cream scoop, place balls of dough into a lightly greased 9-inch square baking pan.

4. Let rise for about 30–35 minutes in a warm spot. Rolls should double in size.

5. Bake approximately 15 minutes, until a toothpick inserted in the middle of one tests clean, and rolls are lightly browned on top.

Note: Did you know that a typical ice cream scoop holds about ¼ cup, which adds shape and makes it ideal for scooping out dinner roll dough?

Dinner Rolls

– Sorghum Flour –
SERVES 9

These plain, light, soft, whole-grain tasting rolls remind me of soft dinner rolls at holiday meals. The flavor of sorghum is very apparent in a good way. I suggest you serve jam with these.

2 tablespoons canola oil

¾ cup sorghum flour, 100 grams

2 teaspoons sugar

3 egg whites, room temperature

2 teaspoons baking powder

¼ teaspoon baking soda

½ teaspoon salt

1½ teaspoons xanthan gum

1 tablespoon (or one packet) yeast, dissolved in ½ cup warm water

1. Preheat oven to 350°F.

2. Mix flour and oil until well combined. Add remaining ingredients in the order given, being sure to sprinkle the xanthan gum around evenly to avoid lumps. Beat until well-blended. Then continue beating until dough feels stiff.

3. With an ice cream scoop, place balls of dough into a lightly greased 9-inch square baking pan.

4. Let rise for about 30–40 minutes in a warm spot. Rolls should double in size.

5. Bake approximately 15 minutes, until a toothpick inserted in the middle of one tests clean, and rolls are lightly browned on top.

Note: Most of the rolls in this chapter will settle a little when cooling. That will not, however, affect the wonderful texture!

Flatbread

– Sorghum Flour –

MAKES 7–8 SMALL WRAPS OR 4 LARGER WRAPS

If you like full whole-grain breads, this flavorful flatbread is the right one for you.

2 tablespoons oil

1 cup sorghum flour,
135 grams

2 teaspoons sugar

3 egg whites, room temperature

½ cup applesauce

¼ teaspoon baking soda

½ teaspoon salt

2 teaspoons xanthan gum

1 tablespoon apple cider
vinegar

1. Preheat oven to 375°F.

2. Mix flour and oil until well combined. Add remaining ingredients in the order given, being sure to sprinkle the xanthan gum around evenly to avoid lumps. Beat until well-blended. Then continue beating until dough feels stiff. Then beat just a minute or so longer to develop additional structure.

3. For small, 6-inch wraps, place ¼ cup (an ice cream scoopful) of dough onto a lightly greased baking sheet, and press into a 6-inch circle using moist fingertips.

4. For larger, 8-inch wraps, place ½ cup (two ice cream scoopfuls) of dough onto the baking sheet in the same manner, and press into 8-inch circles.

5. Bake for approximately 10 minutes, until lightly browned on top.

Focaccia

– Brown Rice Flour –
MAKES 2 8-INCH FOCACCIAS

✦

This super-fast and yummy bread is the perfect accompaniment to appetizers!

2 tablespoons olive oil

1 cup brown rice flour,
   125 grams

1 teaspoon sugar

2 egg whites, room temperature

½ cup water

¼ teaspoon baking soda

½ teaspoon salt

1 teaspoon apple cider vinegar

2½ teaspoons xanthan gum

TOPPING:

2 tablespoons olive oil

½ teaspoon garlic salt

1 tablespoon dried rosemary

½ teaspoon crushed red
   pepper (optional)

1. Preheat oven to 400°F.

2. Mix flour and oil until well combined. Add remaining ingredients in the order given, being sure to sprinkle the xanthan gum around evenly to avoid lumps. Beat until well-blended. Then continue beating until dough feels stiff. This makes the dough a little easier to handle.

3. Divide dough in half. Spread (with moistened fingertips) onto a greased baking sheet into two 8-inch circles of even thickness. Make indentations or dimples in the dough with your fingertips.

4. Prebake for 7 minutes (to set the crust, so it doesn't blend with olive oil).

5. Top with olive oil and other spices as desired.

6. Bake for approximately 15 more minutes until crust is browned.

Hamburger Rolls

– Brown Rice Flour –
MAKES 4 LARGE ROLLS

◆

*The flavor and texture of these rolls will delight you. These rolls
will sink a little during cooling, but that doesn't affect their taste one bit.
And they are substantial enough to stand up to a nice thick burger,
a "Dagwood" sandwich, or anything you want to pile on.*

2 tablespoons canola oil

1 cup brown rice flour,
   125 grams

1 tablespoon sugar

3 egg whites, room temperature

½ cup applesauce

2 teaspoons baking powder

¼ teaspoon baking soda

½ teaspoon salt

2 teaspoons xanthan gum

1 tablespoon (or one packet)
   yeast, dissolved in
   2 tablespoons water

1. Preheat oven to 350°F.

2. Mix flour and oil until well combined. Add remaining ingredients in the order given, being sure to sprinkle the xanthan gum around evenly to avoid lumps. Beat until well-blended. Then continue beating until dough feels stiff.

3. Place ½ cup of dough (two scoops with ice cream scoop) onto a lightly greased baking sheet. With moist fingertips, shape the dough mounds into domes.

4. Let rise for about 30–40 minutes in a warm spot. Rolls should double in size.

5. Bake approximately 15–20 minutes, until a toothpick inserted in the middle of one tests clean, and rolls are lightly browned on top.

My Favorite Flatbread

– Brown Rice Flour, Sorghum Flour –
MAKES 7–8 SMALL WRAPS OR 4 LARGER WRAPS

✦

*This flatbread is just about perfect. It has a soft texture,
accented with an almost-crisp bottom from baking. It would be
perfect to use for fajitas, fish tacos, or an everyday sandwich.*

2 tablespoons canola oil

¾ cup brown rice flour,
    95 grams

¼ cup sorghum flour,
    35 grams

1 tablespoon honey

3 egg whites, room temperature

½ cup applesauce

¼ teaspoon baking soda

½ teaspoon salt

2 teaspoons xanthan gum

1 tablespoon apple cider
    vinegar

1. Preheat oven to 375°F.

2. Mix flours and oil until well combined. Add remaining ingredients
   in the order given, being sure to
   sprinkle the xanthan gum around
   evenly to avoid lumps. Beat until
   well-blended. Then continue beating until dough feels stiff. Then
   beat just a minute or so longer to
   develop additional structure.

3. For small, 6-inch wraps, place ¼ cup
   (an ice cream scoopful) of dough
   onto a lightly greased baking sheet
   and press into a 6-inch circle using
   moist fingertips.

4. For larger, 8-inch wraps, place ½ cup
   (two ice cream scoopfuls) of dough
   onto the baking sheet in the same
   manner, and press into 8-inch circles.

5. Bake for approximately 10 minutes,
   until bread is lightly browned on top.

Breads—Rolls, Flatbread, Pizza Crusts, etc.

Naan

– Brown Rice Flour, Sorghum Flour –
MAKES 4 LARGE NAAN

✦

I love Indian food (I love most foods for that matter!). But I really love the bread baked in a tandoor (clay) oven and served in Indian restaurants. This version, however, doesn't require a special oven. It is great dipped in a little excess sauce or simply used to transport your favorite sandwich foods.

2 tablespoons canola oil

¾ cup brown rice flour, 95 grams

¼ cup sorghum flour, 35 grams

1 tablespoon honey

3 egg whites, room temperature

½ cup applesauce

½ teaspoon baking soda

½ teaspoon salt

2 teaspoons xanthan gum

1 tablespoon apple cider vinegar

1. Preheat oven to 375°F.

2. Mix flours and oil until well combined. Add remaining ingredients in the order given, being sure to sprinkle the xanthan gum around evenly to avoid lumps. Beat until well-blended. Then continue beating until the dough feels stiff. Then beat just a minute or so longer to develop additional structure.

3. Place ½ cup (two ice cream scoopfuls) of dough onto a lightly greased baking sheet, and press into an 8-inch circle using moist fingertips.

4. Bake for approximately 10 minutes, until naan is lightly browned on top.

No-Cook Pizza Sauce

MAKES 1½ CUPS SAUCE

❖

There is nothing better than great sauce on a pizza! Here we're putting the sauce before the crusts, so to speak. This sauce works well with any of the good pizza crust recipes that follow.

1 6-ounce can tomato paste

1 6-ounce can water

1 tablespoon dried oregano

1 teaspoon garlic salt

¼ teaspoon crushed red pepper flakes

1. Combine all ingredients in a small bowl.

2. Mix well to combine. If possible, allow sauce to set for a few minutes.

Note: To make a dipping sauce for breadsticks, it is necessary to cook this sauce for best flavor. Simply cook in a small saucepan for about 5 minutes. It is so good you'll probably want to put it on some pasta, too!

Pizza Crust

– Brown Rice Flour –
MAKES TWO 8-INCH CRUSTS

✦

*Brown rice is such a versatile flour! This crust (like the others)
will remain quite pliable, even when it's reheated as leftovers. The garlic
and hot sauce amp up the flavor a bit for the more adventurous in spirit.*

2 tablespoons olive oil

1 cup brown rice flour,
   125 grams

1 teaspoon sugar

2 egg whites, room temperature

½ cup water

¼ teaspoon baking soda

¾ teaspoon garlic salt

2 teaspoons hot sauce

2½ teaspoons xanthan gum

1. Preheat oven to 400°F.

2. Mix flour and oil until well combined. Add remaining ingredients in the order given, being sure to sprinkle the xanthan gum around evenly to avoid lumps. Beat until well-blended. Then continue beating until dough feels stiff. This makes the dough a little easier to handle.

3. Divide dough in half. Drop onto greased baking sheet and spread (with moistened fingertips) into two 8-inch circles with slightly thicker dough at the edges.

4. Prebake for 7 minutes (to set crust so it doesn't blend with sauce).

5. Top with sauce, cheese, and other toppings as desired.

6. Bake for approximately 15 more minutes, until crust is browned, and cheese is melted.

Pizza Crust

– Sorghum Flour –
MAKES TWO 8-INCH CRUSTS

*I find that the stronger flavor of sorghum works
well with pizza. The flavors of the crust and the
pizza toppings stand up well to one another.*

2 tablespoons olive oil

1 cup sorghum flour,
   135 grams

1 teaspoon sugar

2 egg whites, room temperature

½ cup water

¼ teaspoon baking soda

½ teaspoon salt

1 teaspoon apple cider vinegar

2½ teaspoons xanthan gum

1. Preheat oven to 400°F.

2. Mix flour and oil until well combined. Add remaining ingredients in the order given, being sure to sprinkle the xanthan gum around evenly to avoid lumps. Beat until well-blended. Then continue beating until dough feels stiff. This makes the dough a little easier to handle.

3. Divide dough in half. Drop onto greased baking sheet and spread (with moistened fingertips) into two 8-inch circles with slightly thicker dough at the edges.

4. Prebake for 7 minutes (to set crust so it doesn't blend with sauce).

5. Top with sauce, cheese, and other toppings as desired.

6. Bake for approximately 15 more minutes, until crust is browned, and cheese is melted.

Breads—Rolls, Flatbread, Pizza Crusts, etc.

Pizza Crust

– White Rice Flour –
MAKES TWO 8-INCH CRUSTS

Here is a straight-up chewy crust. Spread it as thin as you like, but I prefer hand-tossed style. The recipe doesn't call for yeast, so this is a super-fast crust, which has a wonderful crispness right out of the oven; it softens when cooling.

2 tablespoons olive oil

1 cup white rice flour, 150 grams

1 teaspoon sugar

2 egg whites, room temperature

½ cup water

¼ teaspoon baking soda

½ teaspoon salt

1 teaspoon apple cider vinegar

2½ teaspoons xanthan gum

1. Preheat oven to 400°F.

2. Mix flour and oil until well combined. Add remaining ingredients in the order given, being sure to sprinkle the xanthan gum around evenly to avoid lumps. Beat until well-blended. Then continue beating until dough feels stiff. This makes the dough a little easier to handle.

3. Divide dough in half. Drop onto greased baking sheet and spread (with moistened fingertips) into two 8-inch circles with slightly thicker dough at the edges.

4. Prebake for 7 minutes (to set crust so it doesn't blend with sauce).

5. Top with sauce, cheese, and other toppings as desired.

6. Bake for approximately 15 more minutes, until crust is browned, and cheese is melted.

Sweet Rolls

❖

Looking for an easy answer to a cinnamon roll?
Here's a great take on the sweet, sticky treat.

3 tablespoons butter, melted

¾ cup brown rice flour,
   95 grams

2 tablespoons sugar

1 egg plus 2 egg whites,
   room temperature

½ cup warm milk

2 teaspoons baking powder

¼ teaspoon baking soda

½ teaspoon salt

1½ teaspoons xanthan gum

1 tablespoon (or one packet)
   yeast, dissolved in
   2 tablespoons water

TO FOLD IN:

2 tablespoons sugar

½ teaspoon cinnamon

½ cup chopped nuts or raisins
   (optional)

GLAZE:

½ cup confectioners' sugar

½ teaspoon vanilla

2 teaspoons milk

1. Preheat oven to 350°F.

2. Mix flour and butter until well combined. Add remaining ingredients in the order given, being sure to sprinkle the xanthan gum around evenly to avoid lumps. Beat until well-blended. Then continue beating until the dough feels stiff.

3. Mix together sugar, cinnamon, nuts, and/or raisins. Fold into the dough. You want streaks of flavor, not a disappearing blend.

4. With an ice cream scoop, place balls of dough into a lightly greased 9-inch square baking pan.

5. Let rise for about 45 minutes in a warm spot. Rolls should double in size.

6. Bake approximately 15 minutes, until a toothpick inserted in the middle of one tests clean, and the rolls are lightly browned on top.

7. In a small cup, combine glaze ingredients. Drizzle over rolls.

8. Serve hot or cold.

Breads—Rolls, Flatbread, Pizza Crusts, etc.

Yeast-Free Rolls

– Brown Rice Flour –
SERVES 9

These rolls are not quite as soft as those light, fluffy dinner rolls that seem to use each other for support when they rise. These will stand alone, hold a lovely shape, and have a wonderful texture when torn apart. And whether your diet includes yeast or not, they are delicious. They are dairy-free as well!

2 tablespoons canola oil

¾ cup brown rice flour, 95 grams

2 teaspoons sugar

3 egg whites, room temperature

½ cup applesauce

1 teaspoon baking powder

1 teaspoon baking soda

½ teaspoon salt

2 teaspoons xanthan gum

2 teaspoons apple cider vinegar

1. Preheat oven to 350°F.

2. Mix flour and oil until well combined. Add remaining ingredients in the order given, being sure to sprinkle the xanthan gum around evenly to avoid lumps. Beat until well-blended. Then continue beating until dough feels stiff.

3. With an ice cream scoop, place balls of dough into a lightly greased 9-inch square baking pan.

4. Bake approximately 15 minutes, until a toothpick inserted in the middle of one tests clean, and rolls are lightly browned on top.

Yeast-Free Rolls

– Sorghum Flour –
SERVES 9

◆

A touch of honey softens the whole-grain flavor of these rolls.
These are great with anything.

2 tablespoons canola oil

¾ cup sorghum flour,
100 grams

1 tablespoon honey

3 egg whites, room temperature

½ cup applesauce

1 teaspoon baking powder

1 teaspoon baking soda

½ teaspoon salt

2 teaspoons xanthan gum

2 teaspoons apple cider vinegar

1. Preheat oven to 350°F.

2. Mix flour and oil until well combined. Add remaining ingredients in the order given, being sure to sprinkle the xanthan gum around evenly to avoid lumps. Beat until well-blended. Then continue beating until dough feels stiff.

3. With an ice cream scoop, place balls of dough into a lightly greased 9-inch square baking pan.

4. Bake approximately 15 minutes, until toothpick inserted in the middle of one tests clean, and rolls are lightly browned on top.

Breads—Rolls, Flatbread, Pizza Crusts, etc.

CHAPTER 6

Quick Breads and Muffins

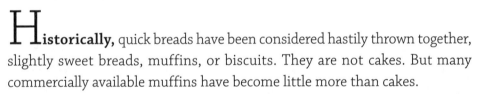

Historically, quick breads have been considered hastily thrown together, slightly sweet breads, muffins, or biscuits. They are not cakes. But many commercially available muffins have become little more than cakes.

I think there is something wonderful that should be cherished about a muffin: It should be sweet enough to tease the palate, yet not so sweet as to be confused with a dessert. Fruit, nuts, or even bits of chocolate can play to your senses. The smell of a freshly baked muffin is unforgettable. These are the muffins you'll find in this chapter.

My favorite quick bread is the Cranberry Bread. There is a hint of sugar placed on top of the bread before it is baked. Again, the gentle teasing is enough to make you hungry.

But there is something else you don't want to miss in this chapter—the biscuits. There are two versions, the first made with sorghum flour and the second that mimics Popeye's biscuits made with brown rice flour. A friend tried the latter and said they were quite buttery and a little salty. Exactly!

Banana Nut Muffins

– Brown Rice Flour –
MAKES 9 MUFFINS

This brown rice formulation may just be the best in the book.
I used just one large over-ripe banana to reach the ⅓ cup of smashed banana.
The flavor is subtle.

¼ cup butter

¾ cup brown rice flour, 95 grams

⅓ cup sugar

2 eggs

⅓ cup smashed over-ripe banana

1 tablespoon baking powder

¼ teaspoon baking soda

¼ teaspoon salt

1 teaspoon vanilla

½ teaspoon xanthan gum

½ cup walnut pieces, chopped (or other favorite nut)

1. Preheat oven to 350°F.

2. Mix flour and butter until well combined.

3. Add remaining ingredients, except nuts. Beat well. Batter will be nicely thick. Stir in walnuts.

4. Spoon into lined muffin tin.

5. Bake 18–22 minutes, until toothpick inserted in the middle of one muffin tests clean, and muffins are lightly browned on top.

Biscuits

– Sorghum Flour –
MAKES 8–9 2-INCH BISCUITS

✦

These biscuits are very tender and have a mild taste.
I find it's easiest to use a fork to cut the butter into the flour. If you work
the dough with your hands a bit, it will be easier to pat out and cut.

½ cup butter

1 cup sorghum flour,
  135 grams

1¼ teaspoons xanthan gum

1 tablespoon baking powder

½ teaspoon baking soda

1 tablespoon sugar

¼ teaspoon salt

½ cup plus 2 tablespoons milk

1 teaspoon apple cider vinegar

TOPPING (OPTIONAL):

1 tablespoon butter, melted

1. Preheat oven to 375°F.

2. In medium bowl, blend all ingredients, except milk and vinegar, to fine crumb.

3. Add milk and vinegar. Mix well until combined into a pasty, soft dough. It will be quite fragile.

4. Pat dough out on greased surface. Cut with 2-inch round biscuit (or cookie) cutter. Place onto a lightly greased baking sheet.

5. Bake for 15–20 minutes, until biscuits begin to brown. Brush with melted butter if desired.

Blueberry Muffins with Vanilla Glaze

– Sorghum Flour –
MAKES 9 MUFFINS

*This is a very moist muffin that becomes extra-tasty with the vanilla glaze.
These muffins have a very pretty domed shape.*

3 tablespoons canola oil

¾ cup sorghum flour,
   100 grams

⅓ cup sugar

2 eggs

⅓ cup applesauce

1 tablespoon baking powder

¼ teaspoon baking soda

¼ teaspoon salt

1 teaspoon vanilla

½ teaspoon xanthan gum

1 cup fresh blueberries

GLAZE (OPTIONAL):

6 tablespoons confectioners'
   sugar

¼ teaspoon vanilla

2 teaspoons water or milk

1. Preheat oven to 350°F.

2. Mix flour and butter until well combined.

3. Add remaining ingredients, except blueberries. Beat well. Batter will start thin. Beat until it thickens considerably (or berries will sink). Gently stir in berries.

4. Spoon into lined muffin tin.

5. Bake 20–25 minutes, until toothpick inserted in middle of one muffin tests clean, and muffins are lightly browned on top. Note that these muffins will rise up and then settle back a little.

6. For glaze, combine confectioners' sugar, vanilla, and water or milk in a small cup. Mix well. Drizzle over tops of muffins once they cool to room temperature (or hot if you can't wait).

Cherry Muffins

– Brown Rice Flour –
MAKES 9 MUFFINS

❖

This is a great alternative to cranberry muffins. Plus, I've added mini chocolate chips, but you don't have to. The unique combination of yogurt and butter makes for a flat-out great muffin that may be my favorite in this book.

¼ cup butter

¾ cup brown rice flour,
  95 grams

⅓ cup sugar

2 eggs

⅓ cup plain low-fat yogurt

1 tablespoon baking powder

¼ teaspoon baking soda

¼ teaspoon salt

1 teaspoon vanilla

½ teaspoon xanthan gum

½ cup dried cherries, chopped

⅓ cup mini chocolate chips
  (optional)

1. Preheat oven to 350°.

2. Mix flour and butter until well combined. Add remaining ingredients, except chips. Beat well. Batter will be nicely thick. Stir in chips.

3. Spoon into lined muffin tin.

4. Bake 20–25 minutes, until toothpick inserted in middle of one muffin tests clean, and muffins are lightly browned on top.

Quick Breads and Muffins

Chocolate Chip Muffins

– Sorghum Flour –
MAKES 9 MUFFINS

◆

This is a moist, not-too-sweet, yet totally satisfying muffin.
The top has a hint of crispness. I think it's a real winner.
You will be hard-pressed to eat just one.

¼ cup butter

¾ cup sorghum flour,
   100 grams

⅓ cup sugar

2 eggs

⅓ cup plain low-fat yogurt

1 tablespoon baking powder

¼ teaspoon baking soda

¼ teaspoon salt

1 teaspoon vanilla

½ teaspoon xanthan gum

½ cup mini chocolate chips

1. Preheat oven to 350°F.

2. Mix flour and butter until well combined.

3. Add remaining ingredients, except chips. Beat well. Batter will be nicely thick. Stir in chips.

4. Spoon into lined muffin tin.

5. Bake 20–25 minutes, until a toothpick inserted in the middle of one muffin tests clean, and muffins are lightly browned on top.

Cranberry Bread

– Brown Rice Flour –
SERVES 9

◆

This is hands-down, my favorite quick bread. I love the traditional mixes in the grocery store made with wheat flour. Those mixes are the inspiration for this recipe. If you are dairy-free, substitute applesauce for the yogurt.

⅓ cup oil

¾ cup brown rice flour, 95 grams

½ cup sugar

2 eggs

½ cup plain low-fat yogurt

1 tablespoon baking powder

¼ teaspoon baking soda

¼ teaspoon salt

¾ teaspoon xanthan gum

½ cup cranberries, chopped

TOPPING:

1 tablespoon sugar

1. Preheat oven to 350°F.
2. Spray 8x4-inch loaf pan with nonstick spray.
3. Mix flour and oil until well combined. Add remaining ingredients, except cranberries. Beat well. Beat in cranberries until batter is nicely thick.
4. Pour into prepared loaf pan. Sprinkle top with sugar.
5. Bake 30–40 minutes, until toothpick inserted in the middle tests clean, and bread is lightly browned on top.

Quick Breads and Muffins

Granola Quick Bread

– Brown Rice Flour –
SERVES 9

I decided it would be nice to do an oat-enhanced quick bread when I walked past my bag of Udi's original granola. Inspiration can be found in many places! This is a very moist, hearty loaf.

⅓ cup plus ¼ cup canola oil

¾ cup brown rice flour, 95 grams

½ cup sugar

2 eggs

½ cup applesauce

1 tablespoon baking powder

¼ teaspoon baking soda

¼ teaspoon salt

¾ teaspoon xanthan gum

¾ cup Udi's original granola (or your favorite gluten-free granola)

1. Preheat oven to 350°F.
2. Spray 8x4-inch loaf pan with nonstick spray.
3. Mix flour and oil until well combined.
4. Add remaining ingredients and beat well. Beat in granola until batter is nicely thick.
5. Pour into prepared loaf pan.
6. Bake 30–40 minutes, until toothpick inserted in the middle tests clean, and bread is lightly browned on top.

Microwave Applesauce Muffins

– Sorghum Flour –
MAKES 2 MUFFINS

◆

These lightly flavored muffins are soft and tender, with a hint of sweetness.

1 egg

2 tablespoons canola oil

3 tablespoons applesauce

Tiny pinch of salt

3 tablespoons sorghum flour

½ teaspoon baking powder

⅛ teaspoon baking soda

¼ teaspoon xanthan gum

1 tablespoon sugar

¼ teaspoon vanilla

Pinch of cinnamon

TOPPING:

Pinch of cinnamon

1. In small bowl or cup, briefly beat the egg.
2. Add remaining ingredients and mix well.
3. Pour batter into two lightly greased ramekins or microwave-safe mugs. Top with pinch of cinnamon.
4. Microwave together on high for two minutes.
5. Gently remove from dishes and allow to cool.

Popeye's Style Biscuits

– Brown Rice Flour –
MAKES 8–9 2-INCH BISCUITS

These biscuits are ridiculously rich, a little salty, and quite buttery, just like the Popeye's biscuits that inspired them.

½ cup butter

1 cup brown rice flour, 125 grams

1¼ teaspoons xanthan gum

1 tablespoon baking powder

½ teaspoon baking soda

2 teaspoons sugar

¼ teaspoon salt

⅔ cup half and half

1 teaspoon apple cider vinegar

TOPPING (OPTIONAL):

1 tablespoon butter, melted

Sprinkling of freshly ground sea salt

1. Preheat oven to 375°F.

2. In a medium bowl, blend all ingredients, except half and half and vinegar, to fine crumb. Add half and half and vinegar. Mix well until combined into a pasty, soft dough. It will be quite fragile.

3. Pat dough out on greased surface. Cut with 2-inch round biscuit (or cookie) cutter. Place onto a lightly greased baking sheet.

4. Bake for 15–20 minutes, until biscuits begin to brown. Brush with melted butter if desired.

Note: For a lighter-colored biscuit, substitute white rice flour for the brown rice flour. It's just aesthetics.

Pumpkin Bread

– Sorghum Flour –
Serves 9

✦

I prefer sorghum flour with purees and/or vanilla. Pumpkin is a natural choice.
Try substituting raisins for the walnuts if you're a fan of raisins!
Enjoy a slice with a cup of tea and some cream cheese!

¼ cup canola oil

¾ cup sorghum flour,
   100 grams

½ cup sugar

2 eggs

⅓ cup pumpkin

1 tablespoon baking powder

¼ teaspoon baking soda

¼ teaspoon salt

1 teaspoon vanilla

½ teaspoon cinnamon

¾ teaspoon xanthan gum

½ cup walnut pieces, chopped

1. Preheat oven to 350°F.
2. Spray 8x4-inch loaf pan with nonstick spray.
3. Mix flour and oil until well combined. Add remaining ingredients. Beat well. Batter will be nicely thick. Stir in walnuts.
4. Spoon into prepared loaf pan.
5. Bake 25 minutes, until a toothpick inserted in the middle tests clean, and bread is lightly browned on top.

Note: For those of you who like to experiment with recipes: I do not think that lemon pairs well with sorghum flour.

Pumpkin Chocolate Cheesecake Muffins

– Brown Rice Flour –
SERVES 9–10

This recipe was formulated at the request of my friend Cassandra! She's a smart one! We both know that chocolate and pumpkin are great together, but adding in a little cheesecake decadence was her idea. What a delicious combination!

¼ cup canola oil

¾ cup brown rice flour, 95 grams

½ cup sugar

2 eggs

⅓ cup pumpkin

1 tablespoon baking powder

¼ teaspoon baking soda

¼ teaspoon salt

¾ teaspoon xanthan gum

2 squares melted chocolate

FILLING:

½ cup cream cheese, softened

¼ cup powdered sugar

½ teaspoon vanilla

1. Preheat oven to 350°F.

2. Mix flour and oil until well combined. Add remaining ingredients, except melted chocolate. Beat well. Batter will be nicely thick. Set aside.

3. Stir together filling ingredients.

4. Gently fold cream cheese mixture and melted chocolate into muffin batter.

5. Spoon batter into lined muffin tin.

6. Bake 15–20 minutes, until a toothpick inserted in the middle of one muffin tests clean, and muffins are lightly browned on top.

Sweet Corn Muffins

– Cornmeal and Brown Rice Flour –
MAKES 7 MUFFINS

✦

This muffin is designed to pair with apple butter or just a little butter.
It is just a hint sweeter than regular cornbread.

¼ cup butter

½ cup cornmeal,
  65 grams

¼ cup brown rice flour,
  30 grams

¼ cup sugar

2 eggs

⅓ cup plain low-fat yogurt

1 tablespoon baking powder

¼ teaspoon baking soda

¼ teaspoon salt

¾ teaspoon xanthan gum

1. Preheat oven to 350°F.

2. Mix flours and butter until well combined. Add remaining ingredients. Beat well. Batter will be nicely thick. Spoon into lined muffin tin.

3. Bake 18–22 minutes, until a toothpick inserted in the middle of one muffin tests clean, and muffins are lightly browned on top.

CHAPTER 7

Soups and Stews

◀◆▶

The soups and stews in this chapter are very diverse. The Basil Fish Soup is an example of how a light soup can be beautiful to look at and very tasty. It is impressive when plated and complex and simple at the same time.

I made the Slippery Ham Pot Pie because it is hearty and is great reheated—perfect when the family comes home on staggered schedules.

The Cheeseburger Soup was made at the recommendation of a good friend. I didn't want to make a gloppy soup (as photos of this soup often suggest); I wanted to make something special. So I imagined what my favorite cheeseburger would be. My answer was a bacon mushroom cheeseburger! And that is exactly what the soup tastes like. I used Colby cheese instead of cheddar for a more understated flavor. It's right on target.

There are several creamy soups in this chapter. The first is a Smoky Asparagus Soup that is both creamy and has bite at the same time.

The Cream of Cauliflower Soup shares the same creamy/bite characteristic and is light for a cream soup. For hearty, creamy soup, try the Cheesy Potato Soup.

And if you like soups with a lighter base, try one of the miso or chicken soups.

Basil Fish Soup

SERVES 2

*Here is a light, fresh soup, perfect as a first course
or great with a hearty roll and salad for dinner!*

1 tilapia fillet (or other
white fish)

4 large basil leaves, julienned

3 cups water

1 teaspoon fish sauce

1 teaspoon soy sauce

2½ teaspoons lemon juice

1 ounce thin clear rice noodles

2 tablespoons freshly grated
carrots

1. Place water in medium saucepan.

2. Add soy sauce, fish sauce, and lemon juice. Bring to a boil, and then reduce heat to simmer.

3. Cut fish fillet in half. Add to broth and poach.

4. When fish is close to done (less than 5 minutes), add rice noodles and basil.

5. Cook until noodles are tender (less than 5 minutes).

6. Carefully remove fish from broth and place into serving bowls.

7. Divide broth between bowls, leaving noodles in the saucepan.

8. Twirl noodles around tines of a fork and divide between the bowls.

9. Garnish with grated carrots.

Cheeseburger Soup

MAKES 6 CUPS

I made this soup at the request of a friend. He wanted "Cheeseburger Soup," but that wasn't good enough for me. Instead, I created this "Bacon Mushroom Cheeseburger Soup," which mimics my favorite type of cheeseburger.

½ pound of ground beef

2 medium mushrooms, diced small

1 small onion, finely diced

½ cup sliced carrots

2 cups water

1 beef bouillon cube

1 baked potato, peeled and diced

½ teaspoon salt

1½ cups shredded cheese (Colby preferred)

½ cup half and half

2 tablespoons bacon bits, plus additional to garnish, if desired

1. In large pot, brown beef with mushrooms and onions. Drain off the fat.

2. Add the remaining ingredients, except cheese, half and half, and bacon bits.

3. Bring to boil. Cook until carrots are tender.

4. Reduce heat to medium-low. Slowly add half and half and cheese, stirring gently.

5. Simmer for a few minutes to allow flavors to blend.

6. Serve hot. Garnish with additional cheese or bacon bits if desired.

Note: To make the baked potato for this recipe, wash and pierce a potato (russet preferred). Microwave it on high for approximately 4 minutes.

Top: Ham and Asparagus Skillet Breakfast, page 38; above: Sweet Corn Muffins, page 95.

Clockwise from facing page top: Sourdough Waffles, page 48;
Cranberry Bread, page 89; Fruitinis, page 36; Scones (sorghum), page 47.

Clockwise from facing page top: Chicken with Black Bean Sauce, page 120;
Sourdough Bread, page 58; Shrimp in Light Cream Sauce, page 157; Basil Fish Soup, page 99.

Clockwise from facing page top: White Cake—8-inch layer, with
Creamy Royal Icing, pages 222 and 233; Poppy Seed Crepes, page 261;
Chocolate Cookies, page 243; Deep Dish Berry Pies, Page 256.

Top: Bonefish Grill–Inspired Mango Salsa, page 15; Black Bean and Fresh Corn Salsa, page 14; Guacamole, page 17; above: Onion Rings, page 22.

Cheesy Potato Soup

MAKES 5 CUPS

✦

This recipe was inspired by the stuffed baked potato soup at the Texas Roadhouse restaurant. It's rich, hearty, and filling. Pieces of country ham from a ham hock may be substituted for the slice of country ham.

4 ounces lean country ham

1/2 small onion, diced

1 tablespoon canola oil

4 medium red potatoes, about 1 pound

1 1/2 cups water

1 12-ounce can evaporated milk

6 ounces cheddar cheese, shredded

1/2 teaspoon salt

1 teaspoon black pepper (freshly ground preferred)

1 tablespoon dried parsley

1. Cut ham into ¼-inch cubes. Add oil, ham, and onion to large saucepan. Cook over medium-high heat until cooked through. Pieces should be a little crispy, almost like bacon. Set aside.

2. Wash and dry potatoes. Pierce potatoes with a fork. Microwave on high for 4 minutes. Set aside.

3. Cut unpeeled potatoes into medium-sized cubes and add to pan.

4. Add water, evaporated milk, salt, and pepper. Scrape bits from bottom of pan.

5. Stir gently but thoroughly. Bring almost to a boil, and then lower heat and simmer (uncovered) for 10 minutes.

6. Stir in shredded cheese.

7. Pour soup into serving bowls.

Soups and Stews

Chicken Florentine Soup

MAKES 6 CUPS

◆

This soup has a light tomato base, shreds of chicken, rice,
and fresh spinach. It is finished with Parmesan cheese,
which completes the flavor.

4 cups water

1 chicken breast, bone-in (approximately 1 pound)

1 tablespoon Better Than Bouillon Chicken Base or 1 chicken bouillon cube

1 14.5-ounce can diced tomatoes, undrained

2 ounces fresh spinach, coarsely chopped

1 teaspoon salt

1 cup prepared rice

½ teaspoon pepper

1 tablespoon grated Parmesan cheese

1. Place water and chicken breast into a large pot.

2. Bring to a boil, and then cover and reduce heat to slow boil for about 20 minutes, until chicken is cooked through.

3. Remove the chicken and allow it to cool.

4. Add remaining ingredients, except cheese, and cook at a slow boil for 10 minutes.

5. Shred chicken into small pieces and return to the pot. Heat through.

6. Serve hot.

7. Garnish with Parmesan cheese.

Cream of Cauliflower Soup

MAKES 4½ CUPS

*This soup allows the flavor of cauliflower to really shine.
Using additional milk, cream, or cheese gives you a cheesier tasting soup.
I will, however, admit to sprinkling on a few bacon bits as garnish.*

1 cup water

16 ounces fresh cauliflower

1 12-ounce can evaporated milk

1 tablespoon cornstarch, potato starch, or rice flour

1 tablespoon butter

1 chicken bouillon cube or 1 teaspoon chicken or vegetable soup base

¼ teaspoon freshly ground black pepper

½ teaspoon salt

¼ cup bacon bits (optional)

1. Place water and cauliflower in a large pot.

2. Bring to a boil, and then cover and reduce heat to a slow boil for about 5 minutes, until cauliflower is very, very tender.

3. Add milk and cornstarch (or flour). Stir well to dissolve.

4. Add remaining ingredients (except bacon bits). Puree with a stick blender. Return to a boil and cook for an additional 5 minutes over low heat to allow flavors to blend. Stir often. Broth will thicken as well.

5. Place into serving bowls.

6. Garnish with bacon bits if desired.

Hearty Miso Soup

SERVES 2

◆

This is my take on a heartier version of miso soup. Real chicken stock has amazing flavor, but it's time-consuming to make from scratch. Here we use the great base flavor of miso and chicken bouillon, with lots of good additions. With a salad or roll, this makes a great quick dinner.

2½ cups water

1 tablespoon dried seaweed

1 bouillon cube (chicken or vegetable)

1 ounce thin rice noodles

3 ounces firm tofu cut into chunks

2 tablespoons Japanese soybean paste (light color)

2 mushrooms, thinly sliced (optional)

1. Place everything into a medium saucepan. Bring to a boil. Cook for just a minute or so.

2. When noodles are tender, put in serving bowls

Note: Japanese soybean paste may be marketed as miso paste. Just be sure to double-check the ingredients list to confirm it's gluten-free.

Lemon Grass Chicken Soup

MAKES 6 CUPS

✦

*This Thai-inspired soup has a bright undertone,
clear rice noodles, and fragrant lemon grass.*

4 cups water

1 chicken breast, bone-in
(approximately 1 pound)

1-inch slice fresh ginger,
cut in half

8-inch length of fresh
lemon grass, split lengthwise

1 teaspoon Better Than Bouillon
Chicken Base or 1 chicken
bouillon cube

1 teaspoon lime juice

2.6 ounces spaghetti-thin clear
rice noodles

8 fresh basil leaves, sliced in
strips (Thai basil preferred)

½ teaspoon salt

½ teaspoon soy sauce

1. Place water, chicken breast, ginger,
   and lemon grass into a large pot.

2. Bring to a boil, and then cover and
   reduce heat to a slow boil for about
   20 minutes, until chicken is cooked
   through.

3. Remove chicken, ginger, and lemon
   grass from pot. Allow chicken to
   cool. Discard ginger and lemon
   grass from broth.

4. Add remaining ingredients and cook
   until noodles are tender. Depending
   on the thickness of the noodles, this
   may take between 5 and 15 minutes.

5. Shred chicken into small pieces and
   return to pot. Heat through.

6. Serve hot.

7. Garnish with additional basil if
   desired.

Miso Soup

SERVES 2

◆

This super-simple miso soup is inspired by my favorite local Japanese restaurant, House of Kobe. Firm tofu chunks and/or fresh spinach leaves would be delicious additions to this soup. You can find miso (Japanese soybean paste) in the refrigerator section of your favorite Asian market. While it's traditional to just sprinkle the green onions on top of the soup, I prefer to give them a quick boil.

2½ cups water

2 fresh mushrooms, thinly sliced

1 bouillon cube (chicken or vegetable)

1 spring onion/scallion, thinly sliced

2 tablespoons Japanese soybean paste (light color)

1. Bring water, bouillon cube, and mushrooms to a boil.

2. Add soybean paste and spring onion or scallion.

3. Return to a quick boil.

4. Serve immediately.

Slippery Ham Pot Pie

SERVES 10

◆

This soup eats like a favorite country stew!
Like the country ham it uses, this dish leans toward salty.
If you are salt sensitive, add the salt just a bit at a time.

1¼ pounds country (smoked) ham shank or hock

8 cups water

1 medium onion, unpeeled and cut in half

1 medium onion, diced (¼ inch)

1½ pounds white or red potatoes, unpeeled and diced (½ inch)

4 ounces lasagna noodles (6), broken into large pieces

1 teaspoon salt

1 teaspoon pepper

2 tablespoons dried parsley

1. Roughly cut ham from bone. Place water, ham pieces, ham shank, and onion (cut in half) into large pot.

2. Bring to a boil, and then cover and reduce head to a slow boil for 60 minutes.

3. Remove ham, shank, and onion. Allow the ham to cool. Discard the onion.

4. Add remaining ingredients, except noodles, and cook at a slow boil for 10 minutes.

5. Shred ham into small pieces and return to pot. Discard bone. Add broken noodles. Cook until noodles are tender, approximately 15 minutes.

6. Serve hot.

Smoky Asparagus Soup

MAKES 4 CUPS

✦

*Sometimes creamy soups can be a little bland, or a lot bland.
Two of my favorite foods—asparagus and country ham—blend together
here for a soup that's rich and flavorful. Pieces of country ham from
a ham hock may be substituted for the slice of country ham.*

4 ounces lean country ham

1 tablespoon canola oil

1 pound fresh asparagus

1½ cups water

1 12-ounce can evaporated milk

1 teaspoon salt

1. Cut ham in ¼ inch pieces (cubes). Add ham and oil to large saucepan. Cook over medium-high heat until cooked through. Pieces should be a little crispy, almost like bacon. Set aside two tablespoons of cooked ham for garnish.

2. Add asparagus, except for 4 tips retained for garnish. Reduce heat to medium and cover; cook for approximately 5 minutes.

3. Add water and scrape bits from the bottom of the pan.

4. Add evaporated milk. Stir well and cover. Bring up to a simmer, and then lower heat and cook for 10 to 20 minutes, until asparagus is extremely soft.

5. Puree soup with a stick blender or traditional blender.

6. Finely chop the retained ham pieces.

7. Pour soup into serving bowls and garnish with ham bits and asparagus tips.

Udon-Style Seafood Soup

SERVES 2

This soup reminds me of the soup my kids and I always enjoyed at the Korean restaurant near our old home. Unfortunately "Noodle Man," as it was fondly known to my kids, has long been closed. The chef would make exceedingly long noodles by stretching and pulling the dough. It was more fun to watch him make noodles than it was to watch a person toss pizza dough! While I have used scallops and shrimp in this recipe, you can use whatever seafood you have!

3 ounces dry spaghetti, prepared according to package directions

¼ pound shrimp with shell on (about 15 medium)

3 cups water (cook in)

2 stalks bok choy cabbage, chopped (about 2 ounces)

¼ pound scallops (I used bay scallops)

4 clams in the shell, washed and dried

4 mussels in the shell, washed and dried

3 mushrooms, sliced

½ full-sized carrot, thinly sliced (or two baby carrots, thinly sliced)

Several sweet onion slices, cut in half

1 teaspoons Sriracha hot chili sauce (or regular hot sauce)

1½ teaspoons fish sauce

½ teaspoon salt

continued on next page

Udon-Style Seafood Soup – continued

1. Prepare spaghetti according to package directions. Drain, rinse, and set aside.

2. Place water in a medium-sized saucepan. Add shrimp (with shells on). Cover. Bring to a boil and cook until shrimp are done, less than 5 minutes. They will no longer be translucent. Remove shrimp from the water. Save the water and return it to the pot. Peel the shrimp and set them aside.

3. Have all other ingredients washed and appropriately prepared.

4. Add remaining ingredients, including peeled shrimp, to the pot. Bring to a boil and cook for about 2 minutes. Place in serving bowls. Serve hot.

Note: If you are starting with frozen shrimp, begin by rinsing them off before adding to them the water. You will remove any icy freezer taste. Also note, the noodles used in this dish are not the clear, translucent rice noodles; they should be the traditional spaghetti-style noodle substitute. I like Tinkyada brand.

CHAPTER 8

■ ■

Chicken and Other Poultry

◆

In this chapter, you'll find a wide variety of methods for preparing poultry. Some of these dishes I dreamed of making from scratch before finally deciding to create them especially for this book. Others, including my Chicken Salad recipe, have been favorites of mine for a long time.

You'll also find remakes of some restaurant and grocery story favorites. I've always wanted to duplicate, in a gluten-free version, Popeye's spicy fried chicken, which just happens to be my favorite fried chicken in the whole world. I hope this recipe brings back fond memories! You can even pair this fried chicken with my Popeye's-Style Biscuits on page 92. My Chicken Tetrazzini recipe is reminiscent of Stouffer's. It includes mushrooms in a light creamy sauce!

One of the last recipes I created for this chapter was inspired by stories I heard—repeatedly—about delicious deep-fried Thanksgiving turkey. I'm not the type to encourage anyone to put five gallons of oil into a pot for just one use, so I take the best a fried turkey has to offer—amazing skin, moist meat, delicious flavor—and scale it down to a more manageable Cornish hen. My favorite food tester and I enjoyed half the hen. She walked out with the other half!

111

Apple and Lime Turkey Burgers with Sriracha Mayonnaise

MAKES 6

◂◆▸

I've always thought it odd that many people just substitute turkey for beef in a burger and pile it high with traditional burger fixings. Poultry has its own personality. I had a frozen turkey burger for lunch the other day and added some lettuce and my special mayo and thought it may have been the best turkey burger I ever had. Then I thought, why not make a fresh turkey burger with my special mayo (and give the roll a little attention, too)? By the way, guacamole is also great on a turkey burger!

SAUCE:

¾ cup regular mayonnaise

¼ cup Sriracha HOT Chili Sauce

BURGERS:

1½ pounds 85/15 ground turkey

1½ teaspoons salt

1½ cups very finely diced, unpeeled apple (Fuji preferred)

¼ cup minced onion

4½ teaspoons lime zest

TOPPINGS:

1½ cups mixed spring lettuce (baby greens)

12 thin slices of vine-ripened tomato

ROLLS:

6 gluten-free rolls

2 tablespoons olive oil

½ teaspoon garlic salt

FOR GRILLING:

1 to 2 tablespoons canola oil

1. Preheat grill to medium heat and lightly grease grill with oiled paper towel to help prevent burgers from sticking.

2. In small bowl, combine sauce ingredients. Mix well and set aside to allow flavors to meld.

3. Wash and slice tomatoes and lettuce. Set aside until ready to assemble burgers.

4. In separate bowl, combine burger ingredients. Gently mix together and form six patties, slightly larger in width than the rolls being used. Patties will be approximately ⅓ inch thick.

5. Place on preheated grill for 5–6 minutes on each side to cook completely; no pink should remain. (NOTE: I do not take a chance with raw poultry. Don't worry; burgers will be moist.) Remove from grill, cover, and set aside.

6. Brush rolls (tops and bottoms) with olive oil and sprinkle lightly with garlic salt. Place center sides down on grill and cook over medium heat until nice grill marks appear, and the rolls become crisp, approximately 2 minutes.

7. To assemble, place bottom of roll on plate and top with baby greens, followed by two thin slices of tomato and one tablespoon of Sriracha mayonnaise.

Note: The addition of apple adds flavor and moisture to the turkey; the salt enhances the flavor of the meat. I chose a solid moisture-producing item (the apples), as ground turkey is very soft to handle. A liquid would hinder the formation of stable patties. The Sriracha mayonnaise is bold in flavor, but it does not overwhelm the burger; it enhances it. The flavor of the assembled burger is quite complete.

Chicken and Other Poultry

Sriracha Mayonnaise

MAKES 1 CUP

This is my favorite sauce for a burger! It also makes an incredible dipping sauce for the Fish Fry!

¾ cup mayonnaise

¼ cup Sriracha HOT Chili Sauce

1. In small bowl, combine mayonnaise and Sriracha.

2. Mix well.

Chicken Lo Mein

SERVES 2

✦

Lo Mein is one of my favorite dishes at my local Japanese restaurant.
This dish is styled after their version, except I add more veggies.
You may readily substitute shrimp, tofu, pork, or beef for the chicken—
just modify cooking time for the meat (or meat alternative).

4 ounces gluten-free pasta, spaghetti-style

1 boneless chicken breast, cut into ¼-inch strips, 2 inches long

2 tablespoons canola oil

¾ cup broccoli florets

¼ cup small carrot sticks

1 cup mushrooms, cut into bite-sized chunks

½ small onion, peeled and cut into bite-sized chunks

⅔ cup diced squash or ¼ cup snow peas

1 tablespoon soy sauce

1 tablespoon sugar

½ teaspoon sesame oil

1 tablespoon water

¼ teaspoon salt

¼ teaspoon freshly ground black pepper

1. Cook pasta according to label directions, until just tender. Do not overcook.

2. Drain pasta and rinse with cool water. Drain. Set aside.

3. Cut and chop all ingredients to appropriate size. Set aside.

4. Heat oil over medium-high heat. Add chicken. Cook until no pink remains, just 3–5 minutes.

5. Add veggies and stir-fry for about 1 minute.

6. Add remaining ingredients and stir-fry until veggies are tender-crisp. Stir in pasta. Heat through while stirring well to coat.

7. Serve hot.

Note: Because small amounts of a diverse number of vegetables are used, a trip to the salad bar may be in order. Be sure to check for cross-contamination by croutons or other gluten-containing foods!

Chicken and Other Poultry

Chicken Pot Pie

MAKES 2–3 SERVINGS

*Here's the classic dish with all of the flavor and none of the gluten.
I've used two 2-cup ramekins to make these pies. While this might be
a homey food, the presentation is absolutely beautiful!
The pot pies refrigerate and reheat very well.*

1 chicken leg quarter
  (leg and thigh)

1 cup water

¼ teaspoon salt

¼ teaspoon black pepper

1 small onion, unpeeled
  and cut in half

1 bouillon cube
  (chicken preferred)

3 baby carrots, diced

1 medium potato, diced

½ small onion, peeled and
  diced

¼ cup frozen peas or corn

½ teaspoon salt

¼ teaspoon black pepper

1½ tablespoons brown rice
  flour

TOPPING:

Pie Crust for Pot Pies (page 260)

1. Preheat oven to 375°F.

2. Place chicken, water, salt, and unpeeled onion in medium saucepan. Cover, bring to a boil, and cook for 30 minutes.

3. Remove onion and discard. Remove chicken and cool. Reserve the cooking liquid. Discard skin and debone chicken. Cut chicken into bite-sized pieces.

4. Measure the broth. Add enough water to equal 1 cup. Return chicken to broth/water in saucepan.

5. Add the remaining ingredients.

6. Bring to a boil over medium-high heat and cook until thickened.

7. Pour into two 2-cup, oven-safe baking dishes or three smaller oven-safe baking dishes for smaller servings.

8. Top each baking dish with pie crust. Cut several slits in crust to allow steam to escape.

9. Bake for 25–30 minutes, until crust is nicely browned and vegetables are tender.

10. Serve hot.

Note: It is a good idea to place ramekins on top of a baking sheet in case the sauce spills over during baking. Frozen soup vegetables (1½ cups) may be added in place of the carrots, potato, onion, and peas/corn.

Chicken Salad

MAKES APPROXIMATELY 2½ CUPS

*Several years ago I was making chicken salad for an event and,
at that moment, I just felt mayonnaise could be a bit heavy. Here, the sauce
is lightened up considerably by using an Italian (or other lighter) dressing
with the mayo. And, as I always like to play with the yin and yang of foods,
I felt the apple and onion would dance off each other with each bite.*

1 cooked chicken breast, diced

1 apple, cored and diced
(Gala is nice)

½ small onion, finely chopped
or one large scallion, finely
chopped

¼ cup mayonnaise

¼ cup of your favorite salad
dressing (I like a robust
Italian or vinaigrette)

1 tablespoon fresh parsley or
1 teaspoon dried, chopped

1½ teaspoons sugar

1. Combine all ingredients. Stir well.

2. Chill and serve cold.

Note: This recipe can go in several directions, depending on the preparation
of the chicken. Leftover chicken, whether baked or grilled would be delicious!
To make a poached chicken breast, simply place the chicken in a small saucepan, cover it with water, put the lid on the pan, and boil for 15–20 minutes
until all pink is gone from the center of the meat.

Chicken Tetrazzini

SERVES 2

◆

Often made with turkey, this is a lovely casserole dish.
By not rinsing the noodles after cooking and draining, you transfer
just enough rice starch to help thicken the sauce.

4 ounces gluten-free pasta, fettuccini style, cooked, but not rinsed

2 tablespoons butter

1 cup thinly sliced mushrooms

¼ cup diced celery

½ small onion, finely chopped

1 bouillon cube (chicken)

¼ teaspoon freshly ground black pepper

½ cup white wine

½ cup half and half

¼ teaspoon salt

1 tablespoon butter

1 cup cooked chopped chicken, small bite-sized pieces

1 teaspoon dried parsley

1. Cook pasta according to label directions, until just tender. Do not overcook. Drain. Set aside.

2. Cut and chop all ingredients to appropriate size. Set aside.

3. Place butter, mushrooms, celery, and onion in a large pan. Sauté over medium heat until quite soft.

4. Add bouillon cube, pepper, wine, half and half, and salt. Reduce heat to low. Stir until well blended and sauce begins to thicken.

5. Add chicken to pan to warm it. Then add pasta. Finally, add the parsley.

6. Stir together for just a minute or so.

7. Serve hot.

Chicken with Black Bean Sauce

SERVES 4

*This is one of my very favorite Chinese entrées. It does require
a few special ingredients, but investing in these very affordable ingredients
is worth it! I find this dish really is delicious with shrimp, too. I never have
extras when I make this dish, whether there are 2, 3, or 4 of us dining.*

2 cups cooked rice

2 cups cooked chicken
(breast preferred)

1/2 each green, red, and yellow
bell peppers, cored and
sliced into bite-sized slivers

1 medium onion, peeled, and
sliced into bite-sized slivers

2 tablespoons oil
(sesame preferred)

1 teaspoon grated ginger

1 clove garlic, minced

1 teaspoon chili paste
(or 1/2 teaspoon red
pepper flakes)

1/4 cup fermented black beans

2 tablespoons rice wine vinegar

1 tablespoon soy sauce

1 tablespoon cornstarch
in 1/2 cup water

1/4 teaspoon salt

1/4 teaspoon freshly ground
black pepper

1. Measure all of your sauce ingredients, as this recipe (like all stir-fry recipes) comes together quite quickly.
2. Cook rice according to label directions. Set aside.
3. Cut chicken into bite-sized pieces. Set aside.
4. Cut and chop all vegetables into bite-sized pieces. Set aside.
5. Heat oil over medium-high heat. Add vegetables and all remaining ingredients except chicken, cornstarch, and water. Cook until vegetables are almost tender-crisp.
6. Add cornstarch/water mixture. Stir well to allow sauce to come together. Add chicken. Cook until chicken is heated through and sauce has thickened, just a minute or two.

Notes: Look for fermented black beans in your favorite Asian market. They come in a cardboard cylinder—about 5 inches tall with a diameter of 4 inches.

This dish is great with shrimp! Briefly stir-fry 1½ pounds of peeled shrimp, until no longer translucent. Substitute the shrimp for the chicken.

Creamed Chicken Gravy

SERVES 2

◆

*Leftover chicken in a lovely creamed gravy is perfect over toast,
noodles, or rice. In classic style, this recipe begins with a roux, a blend
of fat and flour cooked slowly before liquid is added. If gravy thickens
a bit too much, thin with just a bit of milk during reheating.*

2 tablespoons butter

2 tablespoons brown rice flour

½ small onion, finely diced

1 cup milk

1 chicken bouillon cube

¼ teaspoon salt

¼ teaspoon freshly ground
black pepper

1 cup chicken, diced

Thinly sliced green onion or
chives

1. In large frying pan, cook butter,
   onion, and flour over medium-low
   heat until nicely browned.

2. Add milk, bouillon cube, salt, and
   pepper.

3. Cook, stirring, until gravy is thick.

4. Add chicken and stir well.

5. Garnish with green onion or chives.

Deep-Fried Cornish Hen with Fresh Cranberry Salad

SERVES 1–2

◆

I made this recipe right after Thanksgiving because I was inspired by the popularity of deep-fried turkey. This recipe is delicious simplicity at its best! Did I mention, it is also super-moist, has great flavor, and is a new favorite of mine!

1 Cornish hen, between 1.75 and 2 pounds

FOR FRYING:

Peanut or canola oil

1. Heat oil, in a pot or dedicated deep fryer, to 375°F.

2. Wash and dry Cornish hen, inside and out.

3. Carefully place hen, breast-side down, into the hot oil. Do not cover.

4. Fry for approximately 20 minutes to an internal temperature of 180°F.

5. Remove from oil and drain on paper towels. Serve hot.

Helpful hints for deep-frying cornish hen:

1. The quantity of oil needed for frying can be calculated by placing the hen in the frying vessel and covering it with water. Remove the hen and measure the amount of water in the container. This will be the amount of oil needed. Discard the water and dry the frying vessel thoroughly.

2. Do not fry a frozen hen! Hen must be fully defrosted.

3. Wash and dry the hen inside and out prior to frying. This will help limit oil spatter.

Fresh Cranberry Salad

SERVES 4

This simple cranberry salad was on our Thanksgiving table this year. It only takes a few minutes to prepare and can be embellished as much or as little as you like.

1½ cups fresh cranberries

1 naval orange

¼ cup sugar

½ cup water

OPTIONAL:

1 tablespoon Jell-o, cranberry
  or raspberry flavor

¼ cup chopped pecans

GARNISH:

1 tablespoon sliced cranberries

1. Wash cranberries and place in a small saucepan. Peel and chop the orange. Place in the pan. Add sugar and water. Cover and bring to the boil over medium heat. Cook until cranberries pop open. If you cook with the pan uncovered, the cranberries will literally "pop," sometimes spraying boiling juices.

2. Cool slightly and coarsely puree with a stick blender. Add Jell-o if you want the sauce to thicken when chilled. Add chopped nuts and stir well, if desired.

3. Serve warm or cold.

Note: If you do not have a stick blender, chop oranges quite small prior to cooking. And simply enjoy a chunkier sauce.

Fried Chicken Livers

– Brown Rice Flour, Sorghum Flour –
SERVES 2–4

You either love them or you don't. These are incredibly tasty, crisp deep-fried chicken livers. I like to think of them as nature's foie gras.

1 pound chicken livers

COATING

½ cup brown rice flour

¼ cup sorghum flour

¼ teaspoon xanthan gum

¼ teaspoon salt

¼ teaspoon pepper

FOR FRYING:

Peanut or canola oil

1. Heat oil, in a pot or dedicated deep fryer, to 375°F.
2. Rinse off chicken livers, if desired. Set aside. Do not dry!
3. Mix coating ingredients in a bowl until well combined.
4. Cover livers with coating, and press to coat well.
5. Carefully place livers into hot oil. Do not crowd.
6. Fry until coating is lightly browned, and livers are cooked through, approximately 2–3 minutes. No red should remain in the middle.
7. Remove from oil, and drain on paper towels. Sprinkle lightly with salt.

Chicken and Other Poultry

Grilled Dry-Rub Boneless Chicken Breasts

MAKES 2 PIECES

Dry rubs really bring out the flavor in meats. Here, I've used flavors of Thanksgiving turkey, but you should experiment with your favorite spices! If you are careful in grilling, your chicken will be moist and delicious! No pink should remain, but you should avoid overcooking as well.

2 boneless chicken breasts, skin removed

1 tablespoon dried rosemary

1 teaspoon ground sage

1 teaspoon onion powder

¼ teaspoon black pepper

1. Preheat grill to medium setting.
2. Wash and dry chicken pieces. Set aside.
3. Combine all spices in a large zip-type plastic bag. Crush spices with your fingertips to release the flavors. Shake well to blend.
4. Add chicken breasts and press spices into the chicken. Allow to rest in the refrigerator for about 10 minutes (or even overnight).
5. Grill on each side (with lid down) for about 10 minutes until cooked through. Cooking times will vary, depending on the size of the chicken breasts.

Oven-Roasted Chicken with Lemon and Tarragon

SERVES 4–6

*While I often prefer robust and spicy flavors, this recipe
has a more subtle approach. Find yourself with extra broth?
It makes the best gravy for hot chicken sandwiches I have ever eaten.*

1 6-pound roasting chicken

2 lemons

1 tablespoon dried tarragon

1 cup water

½ teaspoon salt

1. Preheat oven to 375°F.

2. Wash and dry chicken. Remove giblets and save for another use (or discard).

3. Place chicken breast-side down in large oven-safe pot or roasting pan.

4. Chop lemons into large chunks. Place lemons and tarragon inside the body cavity.

5. Sprinkle half of the salt over the chicken.

6. Cover tightly. Bake for 1 hour.

7. Uncover and turn chicken over. Sprinkle remaining half of salt over chicken.

8. Bake until chicken is done, approximately 30 minutes more. Do not undercook. Juices should run clear, and meat should no longer be pink.

9. Serve hot.

■ ■

Amazing Gravy from Roasted Chicken

MAKES 1¼ CUPS

This recipe has been written for 1 cup of broth, but you are likely to have more broth than that when roasting a chicken of this size. Just multiply this recipe accordingly.

1 cup of broth

Pinch of salt

1 chicken bouillon cube

1 tablespoon cornstarch dissolved in ¼ cup water

1. Place broth in a saucepan over medium heat.

2. Add salt and bouillon cube. Allow to dissolve.

3. Stir cornstarch in water to dissolve.

4. Add to broth, stir, and bring to slow boil to thicken. Serve hot.

Popeye's-Style Pan-Fried Chicken

MAKES 2 PIECES

I love, love, love the fried chicken at Popeye's. The deeply marinated heat is just so tasty. Here's an easy way to get great hot flavor in little time. If you don't have boneless chicken breasts, other chicken pieces may certainly be substituted. They would actually be a more-authentic presentation, too!

2 boneless chicken breasts, skin removed (or not, if you prefer)

MARINADE:

¼ cup hot sauce

¼ teaspoon salt

COATING:

½ cup brown rice flour

¼ teaspoon xanthan gum

¼ teaspoon salt

¼ teaspoon cayenne pepper

FOR FRYING:

½ cup canola oil

continued on next page

Popeye's-Style Pan-Fried Chicken – continued

1. Wash and dry chicken. Set aside.

2. Combine hot sauce and salt in a large bowl.

3. Cut a few slits in the chicken (to allow marinade to penetrate).

4. Add chicken to hot sauce mixture. Cover tightly and allow to marinate in the refrigerator for about 10 minutes (or even overnight).

5. Combine coating ingredients in a shallow bowl. Remove breasts from marinade and coat well with flour mixture. Do not remove excess marinade from chicken.

6. Heat oil over medium heat (until a bit of flour sizzles).

7. Place chicken, top of breast-side down and turn heat down just a little.

8. Cook covered for 10 minutes on this side, until nicely browned.

9. Turn over and cook uncovered for another 5–10 minutes until chicken is cooked through and no pink remains.

10. Remove and drain on paper towels. Serve hot.

Note: If chicken pieces are especially thick, after turning cook covered for 3–4 minutes, and then remove the lid and continue cooking to ensure crisp chicken.

CHAPTER 9

Beef and Pork

In this chapter, you will find traditional favorites like Pan-Fried Pork Chops, Oven-Roasted Beef, and Stuffed Peppers. You will also find a few recipes that are just a bit different, almost familiar, but not quite. (Don't you love when your favorites become something even better?) A great example of this is Milanesa-Style Steak, which is like a cross between chicken fried steak and breaded veal cutlets, but better. I'm not a huge beef eater, but I couldn't help eating three of them.

I'd also like to nudge you toward the lasagna recipe in this chapter. It makes three nice-sized servings, enough to enjoy with a friend or have a little leftover but not so much that you'll be eating it all week long.

Among my favorite recipes in this chapter is the Pepper-Crusted Burger. It is like a cross between a burger and a steak and cheese sub. It will likely become a favorite of yours, too.

Beef Stew

SERVES 4

Made in an oven-safe stainless pot or frying pan (or a beautiful Dutch oven), my version of beef stew is very light in flavor. If you are so inclined, throw in a pan of biscuits or cornbread to accompany this classic meal.

1 pound round roast or
   stew beef cubes

1 tablespoon brown rice flour

½ teaspoon plus ¼ teaspoon
   salt

¼ teaspoon black pepper

½ teaspoon dried basil leaves

2 tablespoons canola oil

2 large carrots, peeled and
   sliced (¾-inch)

4 medium red potatoes,
   unpeeled, cut into chunks
   (¾-inch)

1 large onion, peeled and
   cut into chunks (¾-inch)

1 cup dry white wine or water

Note: Why should you use wine?
I like the complexity that it adds
to many dishes. Substitute water
or apple juice if you don't care
for wine.

1. Preheat oven to 350°F.

2. Cut meat into ¾-inch pieces.

3. Sprinkle meat with brown rice flour, salt, pepper, and dried basil leaves. Mix to coat well.

4. Place oil in pan over medium-high heat. Quickly brown the meat. Add any excess flour mixture to pan as well. Remove from heat.

5. Wash carrots. Add to pan.

6. Wash potatoes. There is no need to peel them. Add to pan.

7. Add onions to pan.

8. Add wine or water to the pan. Use a spatula to scrape up bits from the bottom of the pan. Return to heat if necessary to help loosen the browned bits.

9. Cover tightly. Bake for 2 hours.

10. Carefully remove pan from oven and place on the stovetop. Remember to use your potholders! Add the remaining ¼ teaspoon salt. This additional salt makes a huge difference in the flavor of the dish.

Beef Tips and Onions

SERVES 4

This is a classic dinner, made with onions and finished with a little sour cream at the end. Wine adds complexity to the sauce, but water or apple juice could be substituted. If you are dairy-free, simply omit the sour cream and allow the sauce to reduce just a bit. The sauce is quite flavorful, making it perfect to serve over noodles.

1 pound sirloin tip steak (cut into ¾-inch cubes)

1 tablespoon brown rice flour

½ teaspoon salt

½ teaspoon black pepper

2 tablespoons canola oil

1½ large onions, cut into wedges

1½ cups water (or half water and half dry white or red wine)

1 beef bouillon cube

1 teaspoon dried parsley (for color)

¼ teaspoon salt

¼ cup sour cream (optional)

1. Cut meat into ¾-inch pieces.

2. Cover with brown rice flour, salt, and pepper. Mix to coat well.

3. Place oil in a pan over medium-high heat. Quickly brown the meat. Add any excess flour mixture to pan as well.

4. Peel and cut onions into wedges. Add to pan.

5. Add water/wine and bouillon cube to pan. Use a spatula to scrape up bits on bottom of pan. Return to heat if necessary to help loosen the bits.

6. Simmer tightly covered for 25 minutes until very tender.

7. Add dried parsley, salt, and sour cream. Stir well. Remove from heat.

8. Serve over rice, noodles, or even mashed potatoes.

Note: I also tested this dish with fresh mushrooms in place of onions and it was equally delicious!

Beef and Pork

Lasagna

SERVES 3–4

◆

I've made this lasagna in a loaf pan, with three sections
of noodles going sideways. It makes three large servings.

4 ounces lasagna noodles

1 tablespoon canola oil

MEAT SAUCE:

½ pound lean ground beef

1 clove garlic

½ small onion

½ teaspoon red pepper flakes

2 cups water

½ teaspoon salt

1 tablespoon dried oregano

1 6-ounce can tomato paste

CHEESE LAYERS:

1 cup ricotta cheese or
   small curd cottage cheese

1 egg

Mozzarella cheese

Parmesan cheese (optional)

1. Preheat oven to 350°F.

2. Cook pasta according to package directions, but slightly undercook it. Drain and set aside.

3. To make the sauce, brown ground beef in a large skillet. Mince the garlic, and finely chop the onion. Add to pan. Add remaining sauce ingredients, and stir well. Bring to a slow boil and simmer for a few minutes to allow flavors to blend. Set aside.

4. In a small bowl, combine ricotta cheese and egg. Mix well. Set aside.

5. Cut noodles into 4-inch lengths.

6. Lightly grease a loaf pan.

7. Layer sauce, then noodles (crosswise in the loaf pan), then ricotta, then mozzarella, then Parmesan (if used), and repeat, ending with mozzarella.

8. Bake for 30 minutes covered; uncover and bake for an additional 10–15 minutes for cheese to brown.

Milanesa-Style Steak

– Brown Rice Flour –
SERVES 4

◄◆►

*Lighter in preparation than traditional chicken fried steak, our version uses
brown rice flour, to give you a wonderful coating reminiscent of veal scallopini.*

½ pound top round roast,
   very thinly sliced (⅛ inch)

⅓ cup buttermilk

1 egg

¼ teaspoon salt

¼ teaspoon black pepper

COATING:

½ cup brown rice flour

¼ teaspoon xanthan gum

¼ teaspoon salt

FOR FRYING:

½ cup canola oil

1. Wash and dry beef. Set aside.
2. Combine buttermilk, egg, and salt in a large bowl. Set aside.
3. Combine coating ingredients in a shallow bowl.
4. Dip slice of beef into buttermilk mixture. Do not remove excess. Dip into coating mixture.
5. Heat oil to medium heat (until a drop of water dances).
6. Quickly pan-fry for about 1 minute on each side, until nicely browned.
7. Remove and drain on paper towels. Serve hot.

Not Your Momma's Chili

MAKES 6 CUPS

I admit it: My mom doesn't make chili. But if she did, it wouldn't be like this!
This chili is not heavy in any flavor; it's almost light and intriguing.
I like the addition of the black beans (for taste, as well as appearance),
but for bean-free enthusiasts, the beans may be left out.

2 pounds round roast

2 tablespoon brown rice flour

1½ teaspoons salt

1 tablespoon sugar

½ teaspoon black pepper

½ teaspoon cumin

¼ teaspoon garlic powder

½ teaspoon paprika

1 tablespoon chili powder

3 tablespoons canola oil

1 medium-large onion, peeled and diced

½ cup white wine

2 14.5-ounce cans diced tomatoes

1 15.5-ounce can black beans, rinsed and drained (optional)

1. Cut meat into ¼-inch cubes.

2. Cover meat with brown rice flour, salt, and the other dried spices. Mix to coat well.

3. Place oil in a pan over medium-high heat. Quickly brown the meat. Add any excess flour mixture to pan as well.

4. Peel and dice the onion. Add to pan. Cook until onions are tender.

5. Add remaining ingredients. Use a spatula to scrape up bits from the bottom of the pan.

6. Simmer tightly covered for 60 minutes, until very tender. Stir occasionally to avoid burning.

Note: Ground beef can certainly be substituted for the roast if you desire.

Oven-Roasted Beef

SERVES 4–6

✦

Like so many of my recipes, this recipe proves that even simple recipes can make very delicious dishes. I like to use a large oven-safe frying pan with a lid so that I can make gravy on the stovetop after roasting.

1 2-pound chuck roast

1½ tablespoons McCormick Montreal Chicken Seasoning

½ teaspoon salt

GRAVY:

1 cup water to deglaze pan

½ cup water combined with 2 tablespoons cornstarch or potato starch

Salt (if needed)

1. Preheat oven to 400°F.

2. Place roast in oven-safe METAL baking pan.

3. Combine seasoning and salt. Press into top of roast; this will be a thick coating.

4. Cover pan tightly with foil or a lid.

5. Bake for approximately 2½ hours until tender. Remove roast from pan and set aside.

6. Place pan on top of stove. (DO NOT PROCEED IF GLASS PAN IS USED! Transfer juices to saucepan first!)

7. Turn heat to high. Add water and bring to a boil. Use spatula to loosen drippings on the bottom of the baking pan.

8. Combine cornstarch and ½ cup water. Slowly add to boiling liquid, stirring, to thicken. Discard any extra.

9. If needed, add a little salt to enhance the flavor. Serve hot.

Pan-Fried Pork Chops

– Brown Rice Flour –
MAKES 4 CHOPS

I've created this recipe for pork chops to mimic what my mom would have made for Sunday dinner or you might find at a local diner. I keep it simple, using just a little fat for frying, and a light flour coating.

4 center-cut pork chops

¼ teaspoon salt

¼ teaspoon black pepper

COATING:

½ cup brown rice flour

¼ teaspoon xanthan gum

¼ teaspoon salt

¼ teaspoon black pepper

FOR FRYING:

¼ cup canola oil

1. Wash and dry chops. Season both sides with salt and pepper.

2. Combine coating ingredients in a shallow bowl. Coat chops well with flour mixture.

3. Heat oil over medium heat (until a drop of water dances).

4. Place chops in the pan. Fry uncovered for 5 minutes on each side. Cook until chops are cooked through, and no pink remains.

5. Remove and drain on paper towels. Serve hot.

Pepper-Crusted Burgers with Sriracha Mayonnaise

SERVES 6

❖

I love bold spices, as well as the flavors from steak and cheese subs. Ground beef provides an always tender and affordable meat; the grill and my secret Sriracha mayonnaise really elevate the flavor of these burgers. The tomato slices and lettuce offer a nice contrast to the sautéed vegetables. The cheese tames the peppery coating.

SAUCE:

¾ cup regular mayonnaise

¼ cup Sriracha HOT Chili Sauce

BURGERS:

1½ pounds 80/20 ground chuck

1½ tablespoons soy sauce

2 tablespoons black pepper (freshly ground preferred)

6 slices Muenster cheese

TOPPINGS:

3 tablespoons olive oil

1½ cup sliced mushrooms (crimini preferred)

1¼ cups sliced red bell pepper (1 large)

1¼ cups sliced onion (1 large sweet onion preferred)

¼ teaspoon garlic salt

6 green leaf lettuce leaves

12 thin slices of vine-ripened tomato

ROLLS:

6 gluten-free rolls

2 tablespoons olive oil

½ teaspoon garlic salt

continued on next page

Beef and Pork

Pepper-Crusted Burgers with Sriracha Mayonnaise – continued

1. Preheat grill to 500–600°F.

2. In a small bowl, combine sauce ingredients. Mix well and set aside to allow flavors to meld.

3. Wash and slice tomatoes and lettuce. Set aside until ready to assemble burgers.

4. In separate bowl, combine ground chuck and soy sauce. Gently mix together and form six patties, slightly larger in width than the rolls being used. Patties will be approximately ⅓-inch thick.

5. Place ground pepper on a separate plate and gently press burger into pepper to coat it. Don't worry if the burger is not entirely covered.

6. Cook burger patties on very hot grill for 3–4 minutes on each side to almost medium doneness. Remove from grill, cover, and set aside.

7. While burgers are cooking, combine 3 tablespoons olive oil, mushrooms, bell pepper, onion, and ¼ teaspoon garlic salt in a medium frying pan. Cook over medium heat until vegetables are soft, about 5 minutes. Set aside until ready to assemble burgers.

8. Brush rolls (tops and bottoms) with olive oil and sprinkle lightly with garlic salt. Place center sides down on the grill and cook over medium heat until nice grill marks appear, and the rolls are crisp, approximately 2 minutes.

9. As soon as rolls are prepared, return burgers to the grill and place a slice of Muenster cheese on top of each burger. Close the grill and cook just until the cheese melts. Immediately remove from heat to avoid overcooking the burgers.

10. To assemble, place bottom of roll on a plate, add burger, and top with sautéed onions/mushrooms/peppers, followed by piece of leaf lettuce, two thin slices of tomato, and one tablespoon of Sriracha mayonnaise.

Note: The addition of soy sauce to the meat adds flavor while providing sufficient moisture for a moist burger, whether it's cooked medium or well-done.

Roast Beef with Red Wine and Mushrooms

SERVES 4–6

◆

This roast is delicious and elegant but quite simple to prepare.
Serve it with noodles or potatoes.

1 2-pound chuck roast

1 tablespoon canola oil

3 cloves garlic, chopped

1 pound mushrooms, coarsely chopped

1 tablespoon dried rosemary

1 cup dry red wine

¼ teaspoon salt

3 tablespoons butter

¼ teaspoon freshly ground black pepper

1. Preheat oven to 350°F.

2. Place oil in oven-safe pan over medium-high heat. Quickly brown the meat.

3. Add chopped garlic, mushrooms, rosemary, and red wine. Use a spatula to scrape up bits from the bottom of the pan.

4. Cover tightly. Bake for 2 hours.

5. Carefully remove from oven and return to stovetop. Remember to use your potholders! Add salt, butter, and pepper. Stir well.

Simple New York Strip Steak

MAKES 2 LARGE STEAKS

◆

Sometimes I have room in my budget for a nice New York strip steak.
Either pan-fry it or grill it outside (preferred). Broiling just doesn't cut it.

2 New York strip steaks
(about 1 pound)

½ teaspoon salt

½ teaspoon black pepper
(coarsely ground preferred)

¼ teaspoon onion powder

¼ teaspoon garlic powder

1. Trim steaks of excess fat.

2. Mix spices together in a small cup. Stir well.

3. Press spices into meat.

4. Place in hot pan (with 1 tablespoon oil) or over very hot grill for approximately 3 minutes on each side for medium. If you must, cook 5 minutes on each side for well done.

5. Remove from heat. Cover lightly with foil to keep warm for 3 or 4 minutes (if you can wait) to allow juices to redistribute. Serve hot.

Sofrito Pork Chops

SERVES 2–3

This recipe is actually a collision of sofrito (a blend of garlic, onion, and tomatoes cooked in olive oil) and mirepoix (a blend of celery, carrot, and onion). The flavors are simple, and remember that the goal is not to brown these bits of vegetables but to gently sauté them into flavorful submission.

2 large or 3 smaller pork chops

1 tablespoon olive oil (for chops)

2 tablespoons olive oil (for vegetables)

1 clove garlic, finely minced

2 ribs celery, finely chopped (about 2/3 cup)

1 carrot, peeled and finely chopped (about 1/2 cup)

1 small onion, peeled and finely chopped (about 1/3 cup)

1/2 cup dry white wine

1/4 teaspoon salt

2 tablespoons butter

Note: If the wine isn't drinkable, it shouldn't be cookable either! Use a good quality table wine, not a cooking wine. Alice White and Crane Lake are two very affordable and appropriate dry chardonnays to accompany this meal.

1. Preheat oven to 375°F.
2. Over medium-high heat, pan-fry chops in 1 tablespoon olive oil until well browned on both sides. Your goal is not to cook the chops, just sear them.
3. Over medium-low heat, sauté vegetables for approximately 10 minutes. I do this in a large oven-safe frying pan (with an oven-safe lid).
4. Deglaze both pans with 1/4 cup of wine. Combine into the large oven-safe frying pan.
5. Bake covered for 20–25 minutes until chops are well cooked. Remove from oven and remove chops from the pan.
6. Place pan back on stovetop over medium-high heat. DO NOT TOUCH THE PAN WITH YOUR HANDS! IT WILL BE VERY HOT FROM THE OVEN! Cook until half of the liquid is gone. Add salt and butter. Stir well.
7. Return chops to pan and turn off heat. Serve chops smothered with sauce.

Beef and Pork

143

Steak Rolls

SERVES 2–3

These steak rolls are made with thinly sliced top round steak (⅛-inch), but any thinly sliced beef would work fine. The prolonged cooking time makes the beef really tender. This recipe is a spoof on my mom's beef rouladen, which is a thinly sliced steak wrapped around a dill pickle and cooked in a spicy tomato sauce. I've toned down the filling from pickle to bell peppers and modified the sauce as well. I hope you enjoy it!

½ to ¾ pound top round roast, very thinly sliced (⅛ inch)

FILLING:

½ green bell pepper

½ red bell pepper (or yellow or orange)

½ onion

½ teaspoon garlic salt

¼ teaspoon black pepper

⅛ teaspoon salt

1 cup water

SAUCE:

3 tablespoons tomato paste

1 beef bouillon cube

1½ teaspoons paprika

⅛ teaspoon black pepper

¼ teaspoon salt

1 tablespoon butter (optional)

FOR FRYING:

2 tablespoons canola oil

1. Preheat oven to 375°F.

2. Wash and dry beef. Set aside.

3. Wash and slice bell peppers. Peel and slice onions. Set aside.

4. Place 1 tablespoon oil in a frying pan. Sauté bell peppers, onion, and garlic salt until soft.

5. Place one slice of beef on a plate. Place several slices of bell pepper and onion at one end of the slice of beef. Roll up. Secure with a toothpick, if necessary. Repeat until beef and filling ingredients are used.

6. Place 1 tablespoon oil in frying pan. Heat over medium heat until oil is hot. Place beef rolls into frying pan. Sprinkle ¼ teaspoon black pepper and a bit of salt over the beef rolls. Brown the rolls on all sides.

7. Add 1 cup water. Cover with an oven-safe lid, and place in the oven for 1 hour.

8. With POTHOLDERS, remove the pan from the oven and return it to the stovetop. Check to see that meat is tender. Remove rolls from the pan and place on a serving plate. Cover with foil to retain heat.

9. To remaining juices, add sauce ingredients. Simmer for flavors to blend and allow sauce to reduce by approximately half.

10. Pour over beef rolls and serve.

Note: To turn this into a genuine beef roulade, substitute a small dill pickle in the center of the roll for the vegetables.

Stir-Fried Beef and Carrots

SERVES 2

This dish is spicy! Enjoy!

2 cups prepared rice

1 pound sirloin tip steak
  (cut into thin strips)

1 tablespoon canola oil

1 tablespoon chili sauce

1 clove garlic, minced

2 cups grated carrots

1 tablespoon sesame oil

1 tablespoon freshly grated
  ginger

1 tablespoon bean paste

½ tablespoon soy sauce

½ cup water

1 teaspoon cornstarch

1. Measure all your ingredients, as this recipe (like all stir-fried recipes) comes together quite quickly.

2. Cook rice according to label directions. Set aside.

3. Cut beef into match-stick-sized pieces. Set aside.

4. Grate carrots. Set aside.

5. Heat canola oil over medium-high heat. Cook beef and garlic until no pink remains.

6. Add all remaining ingredients, except cornstarch and water. Cook until carrots are almost tender-crisp.

7. Add cornstarch/water mixture. Stir well to allow sauce to come together. Cook until well-blended, just a minute or two.

Stuffed Peppers

MAKES 4

This is a wonderful, old-fashioned meal in a tasty container.
If you want to keep some for later, freeze them before baking,
otherwise, your dish will be rather watery.

1 tablespoon canola oil

½ pound lean ground beef

4 small to medium bell peppers, any color

1 clove garlic

½ teaspoon black pepper

½ teaspoon salt

2 teaspoons dried oregano

1 small onion, chopped

1½ cups cooked rice

SAUCE:

1 tablespoon olive oil

1 clove garlic, chopped

1 14.5-ounce can diced tomatoes

1 tablespoon dried oregano

¼ teaspoon salt

¼ teaspoon black pepper

2 tablespoons tomato paste

1 cup water

1. Preheat oven to 350°F.

2. Place oil and beef in a large pan. Brown and break into small bits.

3. Cut tops off peppers and chop; discard the stems.

4. Place peppers in a baking dish.

5. Add remaining ingredients to the chopped pepper tops, except rice (and sauce ingredients). Cook well.

6. Add rice. Mix very well.

7. Stuff filling into peppers and set them aside.

8. For sauce, sauté chopped garlic in olive oil until fragrant. Do not burn. Add remaining sauce ingredients, and simmer for 5 minutes.

9. Pour sauce over peppers, and bake for 1 hour, covered.

Beef and Pork

147

CHAPTER 10

Fish and Seafood

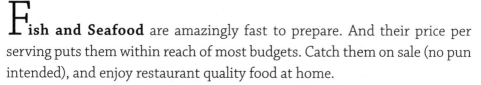

Fish and Seafood are amazingly fast to prepare. And their price per serving puts them within reach of most budgets. Catch them on sale (no pun intended), and enjoy restaurant quality food at home.

If you are a fan of deep-frying, you must try the Fish Fry. I cannot believe how crisp, tender, and moist a fillet of fish can be! I pair it with my spicy Sriracha Mayonnaise, although tartar sauce is always nice, too.

The Shrimp and Asparagus recipe seems like a fancy dish, as does the Blackened Scallops, but they are both super-easy to prepare and demonstrate how wonderful food can be made at home.

Inspired by the wonderful fish tacos at Bonefish Grill, my version combines a simple mango salsa, spiced fried fish, and lightly sauced greens. It is simplicity at its best. Another dish often ordered out is one of my favorite recipes—Stuffed Tilapia. A small container of crab meat and several fish fillets combine for an incredible main course.

Blackened Scallops

SERVES 2

✦

I prefer sea scallops for almost any dish, but bay scallops will do if this dish is paired with the Fettucini Alfredo recipe. Please don't overcook scallops because they get tough very quickly. Using the smaller scallops turns this dish into more of a sauce, while plump sea scallops shine more independently!

½ **pound scallops**

1 **tablespoon blackened seasoning**

1 **tablespoon butter**

1. Drain scallops. Set aside.

2. Place blackened seasoning in a small bowl. Coat one side of the scallops with blackened seasoning by pressing scallops into the seasoning. Set aside.

3. Place butter in a small skillet and bring up to medium-high heat. Do not scorch the butter.

4. Place scallops, coating-side down, into the skillet and cook until seared/crusted on that side. Turn and quickly sear the other side until scallops are no longer translucent.

5. Serve hot.

Note: If the blackened seasoning has not adhered well to scallops, just sprinkle another good measure over the top of the scallops before serving.

Bonefish Grill–Inspired Fish Tacos

SERVES 2

◆

My daughter and I enjoy the fish tacos at the Bonefish Grill so much that I was inspired to try to recreate them. My version of their Mango Salsa is on page 15. And my version of their wonderful, simple salad greens (served alongside) is on page 185. Note: I do not like fish tacos on corn tortillas. Gluten-free flour tortillas are the only choice for this dish! And, if you have no tortillas, try simply plating this dish on the greens, or use one of the flatbreads in Chapter 5.

2 tilapia fillets (or other mild fish)

½ teaspoon blackened seasoning or cajun seasoning

1 tablespoon canola oil

2 flour tortillas

1 cup Mango Salsa (page 15)

Salad Greens (page 185)

1. Place fillets on a plate. Sprinkle seasoning heavily over one side. Lightly press into each fillet.

2. Add oil to frying pan and heat oil to medium (it should be hot but not smoking). Add fillets, spice side down. If fillets are thick, you may want to turn them over to prevent burning on one side. Cook through until edges begin to crisp a little. Remove from pan.

3. Assemble tacos by placing fish, then salad, and then mango salsa inside each flour tortilla. Serve extra salad alongside the tacos.

Crab Balls

MAKES APPROXIMATELY 20 CRAB BALLS

❖

These are so easy to make and are such a great appetizer.
Because there is no heavy breading, the flavor of the crab shines through,
brightly punctuated by the flavor of the Old Bay seasoning. Serve with
Sriracha Mayonnaise (page 139) if dipping sauce is desired.

8 ounces fresh crabmeat

1 egg

2 tablespoons mayonnaise

¼ cup instant potato flakes

1½ teaspoons Old Bay or cajun seasoning

1. Preheat oven to 375°F.

2. Combine all ingredients in a small bowl. Mix well to fully combine. Mixture will become pasty.

3. Roll mixture into small balls, using about 1 tablespoon of mixture per ball.

4. Place on lightly greased baking sheet.

5. Bake until lightly browned, about 15 minutes.

Fish Fry

❖

If you are a fan of fried fish, this is the recipe for you. The fish will be light,
moist, and tender. The coating is barely there, yet it's notably crisp and flavorful!
And my Sriracha Mayonnaise (page 139) is the perfect condiment. Step aside
tartar sauce! If you don't do corn, substitute brown rice flour.

2 fish fillets, tilapia or catfish
recommended

COATING

½ cup cornmeal

¼ teaspoon xanthan gum

¼ teaspoon salt

½ teaspoon cayenne pepper

FOR FRYING:

Peanut or canola oil

1. Heat oil, in a pot or dedicated deep
   fryer, to 375°F.

2. Rinse off fillets. Set aside. Do not
   dry!

3. Mix coating ingredients on a plate
   until well combined.

4. Firmly press fillets into coating to
   cover both sides of fillets.

5. Carefully place into hot oil. Do not
   crowd.

6. Fry until coating is lightly browned,
   and fish is cooked through, approximately 2–3 minutes.

7. Remove from oil and drain on paper
   towels. Sprinkle lightly with salt.

Fish and Seafood

Grilled Mango and Shrimp

SERVES 2–4

*This dish is a winner! If you don't have metal skewers,
place bamboo skewers in water to soak while you assemble this dish.*

FOR SHRIMP:

1 pound shrimp (26 to 30)
  with shells on

2 tablespoons olive oil

1 tablespoon lemon juice

¼ teaspoon cayenne pepper

½ teaspoon dried rosemary,
  crushed

⅛ teaspoon salt

FOR MANGO:

1 mango, peeled and sliced

1 tablespoon olive oil

1 teaspoon sugar

1 tablespoon lemon juice

1. Preheat grill to medium heat.

2. Peel shrimp and place in a shallow bowl. Add olive oil, lemon juice, cayenne pepper, rosemary, and salt. Toss well, and allow to marinate for 5–10 minutes.

3. Peel and slice the mango into ¼-inch slices. Place in a shallow bowl. Add olive oil, sugar, and lemon juice.

4. Make skewers of shrimp and skewers of mango. I use two skewers parallel to each other to secure the mango.

5. Place skewers on grill and cook uncovered for about 5 minutes, turning once. Shrimp should no longer be translucent, and the mango should have beautiful grill markings.

6. Serve hot.

Lemon Crab Cakes on Greens

MAKES 4 CRAB CAKES. SERVES 2

This dish is always a surprise to my guests because the use of lemon (and no heavy seasoning) allows the flavor of the crab to be very prominent but in a soft way. Even if you love traditional crab cakes, I think you will love these, too.

CRAB CAKES:

8 ounces crabmeat

2 teaspoons lemon juice

1 teaspoon cornstarch

1 teaspoon mayonnaise

1 egg white

⅛ teaspoon salt

SALAD:

2 cups fresh greens (spring mix is especially nice, but any softer lettuce will do)

2 thin onion slices

DRESSING:

1 tablespoon mayonnaise

1½ tablespoons lemon juice

1 tablespoon olive oil

1 teaspoon sugar

1. In medium bowl, combine all crab cake ingredients.

2. Place frying pan (with hint of oil) over medium heat. Use ice cream scoop to place four crab cakes in the pan. Flatten them slightly.

3. Turn the heat to low. Cook covered for approximately 5 minutes, until crab has gelled together. Crab cakes may be left "sunny-side up" or carefully flipped.

4. While crab cakes are cooking, wash and dry greens. Place on serving plate. Set aside.

5. In a small cup, combine dressing ingredients and stir well to blend.

6. When crab cakes are done, place them on top of the greens and drizzle with dressing.

7. Garnish with a grind of black pepper.

Note: If you prefer to not use corn(starch) in your diet, try adding ¼ cup of instant potato flakes in its place when working with crab dishes. It is a wonderful neutral binder, and it tastes better than using breadcrumbs or the like. Although I am not gluten-free, I use potato flakes in all my crab dishes.

Fish and Seafood

Shrimp and Asparagus

SERVES 2–3

◆

I strongly recommend serving this delicately flavored dish over Cream of Rice or Grits. They provide a buttery undertone for this special dish.

16 large shrimp,
  about 10 ounces

8 ounces fresh asparagus

1 tablespoon canola oil

1 tablespoon plus 1 tablespoon
  butter

2 tablespoons lemon juice

TOPPING:

¼ teaspoon freshly ground
  black pepper or Old Bay or
  cajun seasoning

1. Peel shrimp. Set aside.

2. Wash and break off tough ends of asparagus. Set aside.

3. Heat oil and 1 tablespoon butter in a large frying pan.

4. Add shrimp and asparagus, and cook over medium heat until shrimp are no longer translucent.

5. Add lemon juice and additional 1 tablespoon butter. Stir well.

6. Serve over rice or grits. Top with a heavy sprinkling of pepper or Old Bay or cajun seasoning.

Shrimp in Light Cream Sauce

SERVES 2

❖

Shrimp is a great last-minute dinner. It also makes ordinary ingredients like broccoli and tomato stand out as gourmet!

4 ounces rice spaghetti-style pasta

Juice of 1 lemon (2 tablespoons)

½ pound shrimp (26 to 30 per pound size)

½ cup broccoli, cooked

1 small tomato, pulp removed, chopped

¼ teaspoon salt

¼ cup half and half

2 tablespoons butter

¼ teaspoon freshly ground black pepper

1. Cook pasta according to package directions. Drain and set aside.

2. Peel shrimp and place in a shallow bowl.

3. Heat 2 tablespoons of butter in a large frying pan. Add shrimp. Cook until no longer translucent.

4. Add remaining ingredients, and cook over low heat until sauce is reduced by ⅓.

5. Add pasta and toss to coat well.

6. Serve hot.

Stuffed Tilapia

MAKES 2 HUGE SERVINGS

If you can find good flounder, that would also be delicious in this recipe. The stuffing is simple and almost pure crab. An extra spritz of lemon juice and a sprinkling of Old Bay seasoning are all you need to finish the presentation.

4 Tilapia fillets

4 ounces crabmeat

1 teaspoon cornstarch

2 tablespoons mayonnaise

⅛ teaspoon salt

1 teaspoon dried parsley

½ teaspoon Old Bay or cajun seasoning

1 teaspoon lemon juice

GARNISH:

Lemon wedges (optional)

Old Bay or cajun seasoning

1. Preheat oven to 375°F.

2. Rinse and dry fillets.

3. In a medium bowl, mix together remaining ingredients.

4. Place two fillets on a lightly greased baking sheet.

5. Place filling on top of these two fillets.

6. Split the remaining two fillets down the middle, lengthwise and lay them around the filling, meeting at the head and tail of the underlying fillet with filling peeking out in the middle.

7. Bake for approximately 20 minutes, until the stuffing is set and fish is cooked through and not translucent.

8. Spray tops of fish with a little nonstick spray and sprinkle on a little Old Bay or cajun seasoning.

9. Serve with a garnish of lemon wedges, if desired.

Thai Shrimp

SERVES 2

✦

Shrimp dishes are fast and easy to prepare and so delicious.
Here, the combination of ginger, lime, and basil creates a great flavor,
offsetting the heat of the hot Thai peppers.

4 ounces rice spaghetti-style pasta or 2 cups prepared rice

½ pound shrimp (26 to 30 per pound size)

5 to 10 fresh hot Thai peppers

Juice of 2 limes, about ¼ cup

2 teaspoons fresh ginger, grated

2 teaspoons fresh lime zest

½ cup loosely packed fresh basil (Thai preferred)

¼ cup olive oil

½ teaspoon salt

2 cups snow peas, washed and dried

1. Prepare pasta or rice according to package directions. Drain, rinse, and set aside.

2. Peel shrimp and place in a shallow bowl.

3. Cut basil into small pieces if leaves are large.

4. Prepare remaining ingredients, as this dish comes together fast!

5. Place half of the olive oil in a large frying pan. Add shrimp and hot peppers. Cook until shrimp are cooked through. Shrimp should no longer be translucent.

6. Add remaining ingredients and stir well. Stir-fry for just a minute or two to allow flavors to combine.

7. Serve over hot pasta or rice.

8. Keep hot peppers for presentation, but DO NOT EAT THEM! They are very, very hot.

CHAPTER 11

Pasta, Rice, and Potatoes

I'm a huge fan of pasta, rice, and potatoes. I could eat these with a vegetable and call it a perfect meal.

Two recipes may stand out as unusual in this chapter. They are Cream of Rice and Grits. These two dishes had to come off the breakfast table and onto the dinner table! We don't quite follow the package instructions, as we'd end up with breakfast food! However, prepared according to our recipes, these dishes become a wonderful base for great toppings! I like to use either of these under Blackened Scallops or Shrimp and Asparagus. Either of these would also be great used beside a nice steak or chops.

My personal favorite potato recipe is probably the Pan-Fried Baby Potatoes. They only take 15 minutes to prepare and taste like a cross between a baked potato and fried potatoes.

If you are a pasta fan, there are two versions of pesto sauce: one with cheese and one without. Both are very good. There is also a Peanut-Sauced Noodles recipe that I fashioned after a Baltimore restaurant's version.

One of my very favorite recipes in this chapter is the Sweet Potato Fries. Baked in the oven, they don't feel so "fried." And with the sauce alongside, they are great! Salt on the fries contrasting with the nutmeg maple syrup sauce makes for one irresistible side dish! It is playful, not decadent.

Cream of Rice

SERVES 2

✦

*I like to use cream of rice or grits as a base for a quick stir-fry
or for some of the shrimp dishes in this book. It is a lovely base on which
to build flavors. The buttery flavor of the rice is accented with just
enough salt to make it a dinner food instead of a breakfast food.*

½ cup cream of rice

2 cups cold water

2 tablespoons butter

Scant ⅛ teaspoon salt

1. In a medium saucepan, place cream of rice in cold water. Add salt.
2. Slowly bring to a boil. Simmer until quite thick, approximately 1 minute.
3. Stir in butter.
4. Serve hot.

Note: When just a bit of your favorite spice is sprinkled on top of the cream of rice, it makes a great side dish as well, especially with fish.

Fettucini Alfredo

SERVES 2

◆

Traditionally speaking, a good alfredo sauce is always
a cream base thickened with just cheese. That can be a bit rich and
even heavy for a lot of people. This version is still quite rich,
but we'll take it easy on the cream and the cheese.

PASTA:

4 ounces of fettucini-style pasta

SAUCE:

2 tablespoons butter

2 teaspoons white rice flour
   or brown rice flour

1 cup half and half

¼ teaspoon garlic salt

¼ teaspoon pepper
   (white preferred)

¼ cup Parmesan cheese

1. Cook pasta according to package directions.
2. Drain. Rinse. Drain.
3. Place butter and flour over medium heat in a large saucepan. Cook until butter melts, and flour takes on a hint of color. We are not looking for flavor, but rather thickening power.
4. Slowly add half and half, garlic salt, and pepper. As sauce is about to boil, add in Parmesan cheese. Sauce will come together very quickly!
5. Add pasta, and stir well.
6. Top with a little freshly ground pepper or even a little parsley.

Note: If the sauce is a bit too thick, just thin with a little half and half. This works even after adding the pasta!

Grits

SERVES 2

❖

So often, restaurants add tons of butter or cheese to make grits tasty.
And they are successful. Instead, though, with just a bit of butter and salt,
grits are a delicious foundation or side to almost any meal.
Plus, you can find them affordably priced in almost any grocery store!

½ cup grits

2 cups cold water

2 tablespoons butter

Scant ⅛ teaspoon salt

1. In a medium saucepan, place grits in cold water. Add salt.

2. Slowly bring to a boil. Simmer until quite thick, approximately 5 minutes.

3. Stir in butter. Serve hot.

Linguini with Red Clam Sauce

SERVES 2

◆

This recipe was inspired by a friend's old family recipe. I've lightened it up just a little, but I haven't sacrificed the flavor. It is still rich.

PASTA:

4 ounces of linguini-style pasta

SAUCE:

2 tablespoons olive oil

1 clove garlic, minced

2 cans clams (6½ ounces each)

1 14.5-ounce can diced tomatoes, well drained

1 teaspoon Old Bay seasoning

Handful of fresh basil, roughly chopped

1 tablespoon brown rice flour

6 to 8 fresh clams (optional)

1 tablespoon lemon juice

1. Cook pasta according to package directions.

2. Drain. Rinse. Drain.

3. Place oil and garlic over medium heat in a large saucepan. Cook until garlic is fragrant.

4. Slowly add remaining ingredients, except for clams and lemon juice. As the sauce is about to boil, sprinkle flour over the top and gently stir it in. The sauce will thicken a bit. Reduce heat to low and simmer for about 5 minutes for flavors to blend.

5. Place clams on top (if desired) and cover. Cook until clams open (just a minute or two). Turn off the heat.

6. Add lemon juice and pasta; stir well. Place open clams on top for presentation.

Linguini with White Clam Sauce

SERVES 2

⟡

Linguini with white sauce is often heavy and too rich. This recipe is neither.
Enjoy the flavor of the clams and the understated creaminess of the sauce!

PASTA:

4 ounces of linguini-style pasta

SAUCE:

¼ cup butter

1 clove garlic, minced

1 cup sliced mushrooms

2 cans clams (6½ ounces each)

2 tablespoons white wine
   or ½ teaspoon vinegar plus
   2 tablespoons water

½ cup half and half

⅓ cup Parmesan cheese

¼ teaspoon black pepper

1 tablespoon brown rice flour

6 to 8 fresh clams (optional)

1. Cook pasta according to package directions.

2. Drain. Rinse. Drain.

3. Place butter, garlic, and mushrooms over medium heat in a large saucepan. Cook until mushrooms are softened and garlic is fragrant.

4. Slowly add remaining ingredients, except for clams, flour, and cheese. As sauce is about to boil, sprinkle flour and cheese over the top. Gently stir them in. Sauce will quickly thicken. Reduce heat to low.

5. Place clams on top (if desired) and cover. Cook until clams open (just a minute or two). Turn off the heat.

6. Add pasta, and stir well. Place open clams on top for presentation.

Macaroni Salad

SERVES 2

*I love macaroni salad. I have taken the traditional salad
from the grocery store deli counter and translated it to gluten-free.
I hope you enjoy eating it as much as I enjoyed making it.*

2 ounces gluten-free elbow macaroni (scant ½ cup measure)

1 baby carrot, finely chopped

3 tablespoons mayonnaise

1 tablespoon sugar

½ teaspoon mustard

½ teaspoon apple cider vinegar

⅛ teaspoon onion powder (or ½ teaspoon very finely minced onion)

⅛ teaspoon salt

1. Cook macaroni according to package directions, until just tender. Do not overcook.

2. Drain and rinse with cool water. Set aside.

3. In a small bowl, combine the remaining ingredients. Mix well.

4. If possible, refrigerate for half an hour or so to allow the flavors to blend.

5. Place macaroni and dressing into a bowl, and mix well to combine.

Note: Depending upon the gluten-free pasta utilized, the pasta may continue to absorb the dressing long after it is mixed. So, please keep the pasta separate from the sauce until shortly before serving.

Mashed Potatoes

MAKES 2¼ CUPS

◆

I forget how easy it is to make great mashed potatoes.
These would be perfect with almost any meal, but I imagine serving them
beside a nice steak or chops for a real diner-type meal! And, I just use a
hand potato-masher! It's so much easier than pulling out the mixer.

1 pound white potatoes

¼ teaspoon salt

⅓ cup half and half

2 tablespoons butter

1. Wash and peel potatoes. Cut into 1-inch chunks and place in a saucepan.

2. Cover with water, and bring to boil. Cook until tender, about 10 minutes. Drain well.

3. Add remaining ingredients and smash with potato masher or beat with a mixer.

4. Garnish with freshly ground black pepper if desired.

Note: I ordinarily gravitate to russet potatoes for ease in whipping up without lumps, but these mashed potatoes are more robust. Yellow potatoes would work well, too. I would not use red potatoes in this application.

Pasta, Rice, and Potatoes

169

Oven French Fries

SERVES 4

*I love the French fries at 5 Guys, but, seriously,
who can eat all those fries? I especially love the fries with Old Bay
seasoning. Here's my easy oven version of those fries!*

1 pound russet potatoes

2 tablespoons canola oil

1 teaspoon Old Bay seasoning
   (or ½ teaspoon black pepper)

¼ teaspoon salt

TOPPING:

Apple cider vinegar

1. Preheat oven to 400°F.

2. Wash and dry potatoes. Cut into
   ¼-inch thick fries, sliced the length
   of the potato.

3. Spread oil on a large baking sheet.
   Add cut potatoes, and top with
   spices.

4. Toss well to coat.

5. Bake until fries are lightly browned,
   up to 30 minutes. Be sure to turn
   the fries about every 10 minutes
   to allow for more-even browning.

6. Place on paper towels to drain.
   Serve with vinegar on the side
   if desired.

You Still Won't Believe It's Gluten-Free

Pan-Fried Baby Potatoes

SERVES 4

These potatoes are a great side dish and only take about 15 minutes to make! They taste like a cross between a baked potato and fried potatoes.

1 pound white baby potatoes

1 tablespoon canola oil

1 tablespoon butter

¼ teaspoon salt

1. Wash and dry potatoes.
2. Place oil and butter in a large frying pan over medium heat. Add baby potatoes and cover.
3. Shake pan occasionally to prevent burning. Cook until potatoes are tender, about 15 minutes.
4. Remove from heat. Sprinkle with salt before serving.

Peanut-Sauced Noodles

MAKES ⅔ CUP SAUCE. SERVES 2

❖

I enjoyed this dish with my kids at the Golden West Café in Baltimore. Unfortunately for the gluten-intolerant, it was made with ordinary wheat noodles. So I decided to duplicate it here, gluten-free, of course! I like to buy small packets of salted peanuts, so I have fresh nuts to chop for the topping!

4 ounces spaghetti-style, gluten-free pasta

2 tablespoons olive oil

2 teaspoons soy sauce

1 teaspoon sesame oil

1 tablespoon sugar

1 teaspoon freshly grated ginger

⅓ cup peanut butter

1½ tablespoons water

¼ teaspoon salt

2 tablespoons chopped, salted, roasted peanuts

1. Cook pasta according to package directions, just until tender. Do not overcook.

2. Drain and rinse with cool water. Set aside.

3. Combine remaining ingredients, except chopped peanuts. Mix well to combine.

4. Place pasta in a bowl. Add peanut butter mixture.

5. Top with chopped nuts.

Note: This dish may be enjoyed on hot or cold noodles. Both are delicious. Just warm the sauce before serving!

Pesto

MAKES APPROXIMATELY ⅔ CUP

*Here's an easy version of pesto. I make it with the food processor attachment
to my stick blender, but any food processor should work just fine!
Toss with pasta or try it over eggs. This version doesn't use any cheese;
it's the salt here that really brings the flavor to life.*

¾ ounces fresh basil
(about 1 cup lightly packed)

6 tablespoons pine nuts

1 small garlic clove, cut in half

4 tablespoons olive oil

Scant ¼ teaspoon salt

1 teaspoon lemon juice

1. Wash and dry basil.

2. Place all ingredients in a food processor and process until smooth.

3. If desired, add a few coarsely chopped pine nuts to garnish.

4. Gently pour olive oil over the top of the pesto to cover. This will help retain its freshness. The pesto is best used within a few days.

Pasta, Rice, and Potatoes

Pesto with Cheese

MAKES APPROXIMATELY ½ CUP

✦

*This pesto is pretty classic in taste. It is perfect to make
in the summer when gardens produce an abundance of basil.*

¾ ounces fresh basil
  (about 1 cup lightly packed)

3 tablespoons pine nuts

3 tablespoons grated
  Parmesan cheese

1 small clove garlic, cut in half

4 tablespoons olive oil

1. Wash and dry basil.

2. Place all ingredients in a food
   processor and process until smooth.

3. If desired, add a few coarsely
   chopped pine nuts to garnish.

4. Gently pour olive oil over the top
   of the pesto to cover. This will help
   retain its freshness. The pesto is
   best used within a few days.

Sausage and Pepper Pasta

SERVES 2

❖

Who doesn't love the taste of a grilled sausage, piled high with onions and peppers? I've decided to bring it to a bowl of pasta for you!

4 ounces gluten-free pasta, any style

4 small spicy sausages, about 10 ounces

2 peppers, chopped (one red or yellow and one green)

1 large onion, chopped (sweet onion preferred)

½ teaspoon salt

Generous ¼ teaspoon freshly ground black pepper

1. Cook pasta according to package directions, until just tender. Do not overcook.

2. Drain and rinse with cool water. Set aside.

3. Cook sausages well, about 10 minutes. Drain off the fat, and cut them into large bite-sized pieces. Set aside.

4. To the pan, add the peppers and onion, and sauté to tender crisp.

5. Add salt and pepper.

6. Return the sausages to the pan. Stir in the noodles.

Simple Milk Gravy

MAKES APPROXIMATELY 1¼ CUP. SERVES 2

✦

Do you ever have some leftover mashed potatoes and just want
a little gravy on them? Drippings from pan-frying a steak, burger,
or roasting a bit of chicken can all be used to make "pan gravy." Supplement
with these extras if you have them, but if not, simple milk gravy is quite tasty.
A bouillon cube can be added to increase the flavor, but it's not necessary.

2 tablespoons butter

2 tablespoons brown rice flour

½ small onion, finely diced

1 cup milk

¼ teaspoon salt

¼ teaspoon freshly ground
   black pepper

1. In a small frying pan, combine butter, flour, and onion. Cook over medium-low heat until thick and browned. Do not burn. It will become fragrant, almost nutty.

2. Add milk, salt, and pepper. Continue to cook over medium-low heat until nicely thickened. Stir constantly to prevent lumps and burning.

Super-Easy Spaghetti Sauce

MAKES 7 CUPS

✦

Some jarred sauces may be gluten-free, but many retail sauces lose their taste under the pasta. This sauce can be easily embellished by using almost anything in your refrigerator—a chopped onion, a shredded squash, some mushrooms, etc. Just cook them along with the spicy sausage. If you have trouble finding loose sausage, buy large sausages and squeeze the sausage from the casing.

1 pound spicy sausage

2 tablespoons olive oil

1 28-ounce can diced tomatoes

2 tablespoons dried oregano

1 6-ounce can tomato paste

1½ cups water (2 6-ounce cans)

1¼ teaspoons salt

1. In a large frying pan, over medium heat, brown the sausage in olive oil. Drain.

2. Add remaining ingredients, and stir well.

3. Simmer for at least 10 minutes. Serve hot over your favorite gluten-free pasta.

Sweet Potato Fries
with Maple Dipping Sauce

SERVES 2

❖

After having a great dipping sauce alongside sweet potato fries at the beach,
I decided to make this recipe! Be sure to use enough oil so your fries get crisp.
The salt provides a nice balance to the sweet dipping sauce.
I wish I could remember the name of the little beachfront eatery.
They gave me extra sauce and told me their basic ingredients. Lovely people!

2 small or 1 large sweet potato (yam), about 1 pound

2 tablespoons olive oil

½ teaspoon freshly ground sea salt

1. Preheat oven 425°F.

2. Wash and dry sweet potatoes. Cut into long "fries," approximately ¼-inch wide.

3. Place into a shallow, oven-safe baking dish (metal preferred).

4. Pour olive oil over fries, and toss to coat.

5. Bake until tender on the inside and crisp on the outside, approximately 20 minutes.

6. Remove from pan, and sprinkle liberally with sea salt.

7. Serve hot with dipping sauce.

Maple Dipping Sauce

¼ cup maple syrup

3 tablespoons brown sugar

¼ teaspoon pumpkin pie spice or nutmeg

1. Combine dipping sauce ingredients in a microwave-safe cup.

2. Microwave on high for approximately 30 seconds.

3. Stir well so that brown sugar fully dissolves. Sauce will be quite hot and should cool to room temperature before using.

Twice-Baked Sweet Potatoes

MAKES 4 STUFFED HALF POTATOES

I love the soufflé-style sweet potatoes served in many homes on Thanksgiving. These twice-baked potatoes are a little sweet, but they're not as sweet as the dish that inspired them! Add a little more sugar if you want the sweetness of the original. If you're not into marshmallows, I suggest a little extra brown sugar and nuts sprinkled on the top prior to baking.

2 small (small baked potato size) sweet potatoes (yam), about 1 pound

Nonstick spray or 1 teaspoon olive oil

1 tablespoon butter

3 tablespoons brown sugar

2 tablespoons chopped pecans (or other favorite nut)

⅛ teaspoon cinnamon or nutmeg

1 egg, beaten

½ cup mini marshmallows

1. Preheat oven 375°F.

2. Wash and dry sweet potatoes. Prick with a fork and microwave on high for approximately 8 minutes, until tender.

3. Cut potatoes in half and scoop out most of the flesh, leaving a thin perimeter. Place the pulp in a small bowl.

4. Spray the outside of the potato shells with nonstick spray. Place shells, cavity-side up, in a shallow, oven-safe baking dish (metal preferred).

5. Add remaining ingredients, except egg and marshmallows to sweet potatoes. Slowly add egg while mixing (or smashing) sweet potato pulp. A mixer will make for a lighter dish. Try to avoid making the sweet potato mixture soupy. (But if you do, don't worry; just don't fill the shells quite as full or they will spill over.)

6. Bake until the filling is set, between 15–20 minutes.

7. Top with marshmallows, and bake until lightly browned, about 4 minutes.

8. Serve warm.

CHAPTER 12

Vegetables

o me, **perfect vegetables** are not overcooked or drowned in sauces that hide their flavor. Often I like to simply steam or lightly boil vegetables until they are tender-crisp. I then drain them and sprinkle on a bit of sea salt or garlic salt.

When you want something more, however, a special sauce or simple pan-frying can be amazing! The Brussels Sprouts in Lemon Dill Cream Sauce or the Stir-Fried Snow Peas are perfect examples of this! Tempura Veggies served piping hot are so amazing.

Vegetables can be transformed into great vegetarian main dishes, too. Reviews of the Black Bean Burgers were very positive. The Vegetarian Chili is also quite nice. My children often eat a vegetarian diet, and with these two recipes, I'm happy to join them.

Black Bean Burgers

MAKES 4 LARGE BURGERS OR 8 SLIDER-SIZE BURGERS

More and more vegetarian options are creeping into family gatherings. Here's my version of black bean burgers. Made from everyday staples, these are a very tasty meat alternative! I find these burgers are especially good with Dijon-style mustard.

1 15.5-ounce can black beans

½ regular carrot or
   2 baby carrots

¼ cup water

¼ green or red bell pepper

6 small mushrooms

½ small onion

1 egg

½ cup instant potato flakes

¼ teaspoon black pepper

½ teaspoon salt

¼ teaspoon garlic powder

1. Rinse and drain black beans. Place them in a large bowl and smash with a potato masher or puree with a food processor. Place mashed beans in a medium bowl.

2. Finely chop or puree carrot, bell pepper, mushrooms, and onion. Add to bowl with beans. Add remaining ingredients and mix well. Mixture will come together nicely.

3. For each large burger, place ½ cup of mixture in the palm of your hand and shape into a patty. For small burgers, place ¼ cup of mixture into the palm of your hand and shape into a patty.

4. Place into lightly greased frying pan and cook over medium heat (covered) for 5 minutes on each side.

5. Serve hot as you would any burger.

Note: Do not freeze these burgers uncooked as they will lose their shape and texture. Just pan-fry and then freeze them. You can reheat them later.

Bonefish Grill–Inspired Salad Greens

SERVES 2–3

This is my version of the simple, delicious, salad greens served on and alongside the Fish Tacos (and other dishes) at the Bonefish Grill. Note: When placing greens on tacos, I like to julienne 1 cup of this salad before placing it on the tacos. The rest I leave in larger pieces and serve alongside.

3 cups freshly washed spring mix salad greens

3 very thin slices of onion

DRESSING:

1½ tablespoons lemon juice

1 tablespoon canola oil

1 tablespoon sugar

⅛ teaspoon black pepper

1. Place greens and onion in a mixing bowl.

2. In a separate cup, combine dressing ingredients. Stir well to combine.

3. Pour dressing over salad just before serving. Save extra dressing, if any, for another time.

Brussels Sprouts
in Lemon Dill Cream Sauce

SERVES 2–3

This recipe is just amazing. It may just convince people who hate Brussels sprouts to change their minds! I know my guest kept eating them until they were gone! This recipe could become a holiday standard.

8 ounces fresh Brussels sprouts

½ cup water

2 tablespoons butter

¼ teaspoon dill

½ teaspoon lemon juice

¼ cup half and half

1. Wash Brussels sprouts. Place them in a small frying pan with water. Cover.

2. Cook over medium heat until sprouts are tender. Keep an eye on them to be sure the water doesn't boil away! Add a little more if necessary. Drain sprouts once tender. Set sprouts aside in a separate dish.

3. Add remaining ingredients to the pan, and return it to low heat. Cook until well combined, stirring often. A whisk would be good for this purpose.

4. Add sprouts back to sauce, and gently stir to coat well.

5. Serve hot.

Brussels Sprouts with Parmesan

SERVES 2–3

◆

This recipe is quick and easy. I like to look for small, exceedingly fresh Brussels sprouts. This dish will be prettier if you don't try to melt the cheese, just let it be a last-minute enhancer.

8 ounces fresh Brussels sprouts

½ cup water

2 tablespoons butter

1 tablespoon Parmesan cheese

⅛ teaspoon freshly ground black pepper

⅛ teaspoon freshly ground sea salt

1. Wash Brussels sprouts. Place them in a small frying pan with water.
2. Cook over medium heat until sprouts are tender. Keep an eye on them to be sure the water doesn't boil away! Add a little more if necessary. Drain sprouts once tender.
3. Add butter to pan of sprouts. Cook until melted.
4. Add Parmesan cheese, pepper, and salt. Toss lightly.
5. Serve right away.

Cream Cheese Sauce

MAKES 1½ CUPS

While not a vegetable itself, this sauce is great as an accompaniment to vegetables. It's also good on pasta and seafood. I have styled this sauce after one of my very favorite cheeses—Boursin black pepper cheese.

2 tablespoons brown rice flour

2 tablespoons butter

1 cup milk

4 ounces cream cheese

½ teaspoon freshly ground black pepper

¼ teaspoon salt

1. Combine flour and butter in a medium saucepan. Cook over medium heat until lightly browned.

2. Slowly add milk, while whisking to avoid lumps.

3. Add remaining ingredients and continue to simmer for a few minutes to develop flavor.

4. Serve hot.

Note: I believe this sauce requires a bit of extra salt if it's paired with pasta. Use as is for vegetables.

Fire Corn on the Cob

SERVES 2

Normally, I love butter on corn, but hot sauce is truly amazing!
Mayonnaise tempers the fire of the hot sauce, and the garlic salt is a natural.
I happen to think the pepper is a pretty finishing touch.

2 ears corn, unshucked

2 teaspoons mayonnaise

2 teaspoons hot sauce

⅛ teaspoon garlic salt

⅛ teaspoon black pepper

1. Peel husks back. Spread on mayonnaise (as thinly as possible), a generous amount of hot sauce, garlic salt, and pepper.

2. Cook for 3 minutes (1½ minutes per ear) in the microwave. You could also cook these on a hot grill until the corn is tender, approximately 5 minutes each side if the grill is open, or 7 minutes if the grill is closed.

Peanut Slaw

MAKES 2½ CUPS

◆

*My kids and I had a great trip to the beach and had the opportunity to
try a lot of vegetarian dishes, including an Asian-inspired slaw. Peanut flavor
from both the sauce and freshly chopped peanuts added to its appeal!
While my version tastes very similar to the original, I think the beach air
and great company made the beach version more memorable.*

2 cups freshly grated cabbage
(about 1 pound)

3 tablespoons apple cider
vinegar

3 tablespoons peanut butter

1½ tablespoons oil

1½ tablespoon sugar

¼ teaspoon salt

½ cup chopped peanuts

1. Wash and grate the cabbage. Place
in a medium serving bowl.

2. Mix remaining ingredients, except
for peanuts. Mix well to combine.

3. Pour over cabbage, and mix well.

4. Pour chopped peanuts over slaw,
and toss before serving.

Stir-Fried Cabbage

SERVES 4

Have you ever noticed that cabbage is either served raw (delicious) or cooked to near-mush (also delicious)? The simple ingredients and quick stir-fry method here make for a dish that's neither too crisp nor too soft, giving it real standing as a side dish. If it is available near you, baby bok choy is especially tender and is even better in this recipe.

1 pound cabbage, cut into large pieces (about 4 cups loosely packed) or baby bok choy, cut into large pieces

2 tablespoons canola oil

1 tablespoon soy sauce

1 teaspoon sugar

¼ teaspoon freshly ground black pepper

⅛ teaspoon salt

1. Wash and chop cabbage.

2. Heat pan over medium heat. Add oil. Carefully add cabbage. (The oil may splatter a bit because of moisture remaining on the cabbage.) Quickly add remaining ingredients.

3. Stir (or toss) continually for about 2 minutes, until cabbage has a bit of color and is heated through. We are looking for tender-crisp. Baby bok choy will take just a minute or so to cook.

Note: This would make a great main dish with the addition of firm tofu cubes, leftover ham, or leftover chicken.

Vegetables

191

Stir-Fried Snow Peas

MAKES 2 LARGE 1-CUP SERVINGS

◆

These pretty little flat pods are always an attractive, tasty dish.
The quick infusion of sesame and soy gives this dish an Asian influence.
I would serve this alongside any fish that is simply prepared.

2 cups fresh snow peas

1 tablespoon sesame oil

1 teaspoon soy sauce

1. Wash and drain peas.

2. Heat pan over medium heat. Add oil. Carefully add peas. (The oil may splatter a bit because of moisture remaining on the peas.) Add soy sauce.

3. Stir (or toss) continually for no more than 1 minute, until peas are heated through. They should remain tender-crisp.

Note: Some snow peas have a tough string that runs along one side of the pod. If yours do, simply grab one end and pull along the side of the pod to remove it.

Tempura Veggies

– Brown Rice Flour, Sorghum Flour –
SERVES 4

I was working on developing a lighter batter and was delighted when this recipe turned out to be so much more! No worries if you are dairy-free; this is also wonderful with plain almond milk.

1 sweet onion, peeled and cut into rings

8 ounces mushrooms, cut into bite-sized pieces

½ pound green beans, ends trimmed

BATTER

½ cup brown rice flour

¼ cup sorghum flour

2 egg whites

¼ teaspoon xanthan gum

¼ teaspoon salt

¼ teaspoon black pepper

1/8 teaspoon baking soda

¼ cup milk

FOR FRYING:

Peanut or canola oil

1. Heat oil, in a pot or dedicated deep fryer, to 375°F.

2. Mix batter ingredients until well combined. Beat until batter is very smooth.

3. Dip vegetables into batter, and then carefully place into hot oil. Do not crowd.

4. Fry until coating is lightly browned, and veggies are desired doneness. I like the mushrooms cooked through, with green beans and onion slices a bit tender-crisp.

5. Remove from oil and drain on paper towels. Sprinkle lightly with salt.

Note: Try this recipe with your other favorite vegetables! Broccoli, squash, thinly sliced yams, etc. would all be great. Batter coats best on well-dried vegetables.

Vegetables

Tomato Salad

SERVES 2

*When summer is long and ripe tomatoes are still abundant,
sometimes we wonder what to do with them. Maybe we just
need a little inspiration. Using lime and olive oil in the dressing
brightens the flavor of this simple tomato salad.
The flavors play well together.*

2 small tomatoes, chopped

2 tablespoons minced onion

DRESSING:

1½ tablespoons olive oil

1 tablespoon lime juice

Pinch of salt

1 teaspoon sugar

1. Wash, dry, and chop tomatoes. Place in a small bowl.

2. Finely chop onion and add to bowl.

3. Add dressing ingredients to bowl and mix well. If possible, allow to marinate for at least half an hour, so that flavors will blend.

Un-Ratatouille

SERVES 4

✦

I am a fan of traditional ratatouille, but the softness of the vegetables doesn't appeal to everyone. I created this combination of vegetables without "overcooking" them with quite delicious results. Please note that quantities of all ingredients in this recipe may be changed substantially. There is no reason to not use an entire veggie!

1 small eggplant
(a mini eggplant would
be perfect)

1 small squash (yellow or green)

1 sweet bell pepper
(red or yellow preferred)

1 tomato

1 tablespoon olive oil

¼ teaspoon garlic salt

½ teaspoon oregano

1 tablespoon lemon juice

1. Wash and chop all vegetables.
2. Remove seeds and stems from peppers and most of the seeds and juice from tomato.
3. Place oil in a large frying pan. Heat over medium heat.
4. Add all vegetables, except tomato and lemon juice. Add garlic salt and oregano. Cook until tender-crisp. Add tomato and lemon juice until just heated through.
5. Serve hot.

Vegetarian Chili

MAKES 8–9 CUPS

✦

Here's a simple recipe with a complex flavor.
Vegetarian or not, I believe you will enjoy this dish!

1 medium onion chopped

½ bell pepper, any color

1 carrot

2 15.5-ounce cans black beans

1 14.5-ounce can diced
   tomatoes

2 teaspoons chili powder

½ teaspoon garlic salt

⅛ teaspoon cayenne powder

1½ teaspoons sugar

1 tablespoon tomato paste

1. Peel and finely dice the onion. Wash, seed, and finely chop bell pepper. Wash and grate or finely chop carrot.

2. Place olive oil and chopped vegetables in a large saucepan. Cook over medium heat until tender, about 10 minutes.

3. Drain and rinse black beans. Add beans and remaining ingredients, and bring to the boil. Simmer for at least 5 minutes.

4. If thicker consistency is desired, smash some of the beans with a potato masher.

5. Serve hot.

CHAPTER 13

Cakes

There just wasn't enough room in this chapter to give you all the cakes I wanted to make, but I promise to make you hungry with these!

I've designed the recipes in this chapter to yield a single 8-inch round cake. Often, a standard recipe produces much more cake than is needed on an occasion, which results in either overeating or waste. I hope this size will suit your gatherings. If not, you can always make two layers with just a little extra effort.

True to traditional recipes, the pound cakes are the most dense with the tightest crumb. They are quite tasty as written, but they would do well sliced and served with berries and whipped cream, too. In the spring I enjoy pound cake served with fresh-picked strawberries.

The Carrot Cake and Pumpkin Spice Cake share similar texture and moistness, with a more open, moist crumb. Both are very good. If you like one, I urge you to try the other as well.

The Butter Cake in this chapter is very interesting. It is surprising that such a small amount of butter creates such a lovely buttery flavor. Soft and squishy cakes also abound in this chapter. They are perfect for a birthday party, and no one except you is likely to know they are gluten-free.

And finally, for your convenience, I've included the smaller 8-inch wedding cake layers from the next chapter here. They're so good, you don't need a special occasion to make them!

Gluten-Free Food Theory: Two ways to make a favorite cake recipe gluten-free

OPTION 1

Start with a favorite recipe (say grandma's famous Eggnog Pound Cake) and substitute a mild-tasting gluten-free flour blend for the flour. Add an extra egg. Increase the raising agent a bit. Add some xanthan gum. Bake.

If the result is too dry, reduce the amount of flour. If it is too crumbly, increase the xanthan gum. If it is dry, switch fat to oil. If cake falls, reduce (yes, reduce) raising agent. Bake. Continue to adjust ingredients and test over and over again.

Note: All-purpose wheat flour ratios/formulations are much more forgiving in traditional recipes than in gluten-free baking; that is why it is difficult to know whether to substitute the same quantity of a flour blend or just a bit less—rarely more.

OPTION 2

Take that same favorite recipe and remember how that cake tasted. Compare it in your mind to your favorite gluten-free (tried and true) pound cake recipe. You might recall it was a little sweeter, had a vanilla undertone, or had a hint of nutmeg on it. Plus, it had just a drizzle of eggnog-nutmeg icing on top.

Next, take that favorite gluten-free pound cake recipe (perhaps the vanilla pound cake in this book), and make a few changes. First, take out the yogurt and substitute an equal amount of eggnog in its place. Perhaps we may add just a bit of vinegar to make up for the likely difference in acidity between yogurt and eggnog, maybe not. Recognizing that the eggnog is sweet, we will not increase the amount of sugar, as that would increase the overall sweetness of the cake. We will omit the vanilla, so that the flavor of the eggnog shines through. Add ½ teaspoon of nutmeg to achieve that reminiscent flavor. And create an easy glaze by combining ½ cup of confectioners' sugar, 1 tablespoon eggnog, and perhaps a pinch of nutmeg. Chances are, you will be right on target— first try.

We all love the idea of keeping cherished family recipes, but by the time we make all the changes, we really have a memory of that recipe. And with the second approach, we get to enjoy that memory sooner with less waste. Both labors of love will honor grandma's recipe.

And, by the way, I finally made that imaginary Egg Nog Pound Cake (page 205). It received rave reviews.

Applesauce Cake

– Brown Rice Flour –
SERVES 9

❖

This rich, moist cake has a flavor of fall that can be enjoyed year-round.

¼ cup canola oil

¾ cup brown rice flour,
  100 grams

½ cup sugar

2 eggs

½ cup applesauce

1 tablespoon baking powder

1 teaspoon baking soda

¼ teaspoon salt

¾ teaspoon cinnamon

¾ teaspoon vanilla

1 teaspoon vinegar

½ teaspoon xanthan gum

1. Preheat oven to 350°F.

2. Mix flour and oil until well combined.

3. Add remaining ingredients. Beat until well blended.

4. Pour into 8- or 9-inch round or square pan that has been prepared with nonstick cooking spray.

5. Bake 20–25 minutes, until a toothpick inserted in the middle tests clean, and cake is lightly browned on top.

Butter Cake

– Brown Rice Flour –
SERVES 9

Brown rice allows the flavor of butter to ooze through! A tight crumb is provided by using plain yogurt. It is amazing that such a light, tender cake can be achieved with so few ordinary ingredients, carefully combined.

¼ cup butter

¾ cup brown rice flour, 95 grams

½ cup sugar

2 eggs

½ cup plain low-fat yogurt

1 tablespoon baking powder

¼ teaspoon baking soda

¼ teaspoon salt

1 teaspoon vanilla

½ teaspoon xanthan gum

1. Preheat oven to 350°F.

2. Mix flour and butter until well combined.

3. Add remaining ingredients. Beat until well blended.

4. Pour into a lightly greased 8- or 9-inch round or square pan.

5. Bake 20–25 minutes, until a toothpick inserted in the middle tests clean, and cake is lightly browned on top.

Carrot Cake

❖

I thought it would be great to make a carrot cake using only staples you always find in the pantry. I am so guilty of finding wilted carrots in the vegetable drawer of my refrigerator. So, when you're buying canned vegetables, grab a can of carrots and a small can of crushed pineapple so you'll be ready when you need a great cake with little fuss. This cake is flat-topped, delicately spiced, and moist. As my friend, Eileen, said, "That's a good cake."

¼ cup canola oil

¾ cup brown rice flour, 100 grams

½ cup sugar

2 eggs

½ cup pureed carrots (see note)

¼ cup crushed pineapple

1 tablespoon baking powder

1 teaspoon baking soda

¼ teaspoon salt

¼ teaspoon cinnamon

⅛ teaspoon nutmeg

⅛ teaspoon ginger

½ teaspoon vanilla

1 teaspoon apple cider vinegar

½ teaspoon xanthan gum

1. Preheat oven to 350°F.

2. Mix flour and oil until well combined.

3. Add remaining ingredients. Beat until well blended.

4. Pour into a lightly greased 8-inch round pan.

5. Bake 20–25 minutes, until a toothpick inserted in the middle tests clean, and cake is lightly browned on top.

Note: One 14.5-ounce can of sliced carrots drained and pureed or smashed with a potato masher nets 1 cup of pureed carrots.

Cakes

Chocolate Cake—8-inch layer

– White Rice Flour –
SERVES 9

✦

This chocolate cake is delicate in taste and texture
but easy in form and would be lovely for a wedding cake.
Be careful in measuring the raising agents, as too much
will cause the cake to sink. (Although contrary to
what makes sense at first, it is absolutely true!)

¼ cup canola oil

⅔ cup white rice flour,
   100 grams

¼ cup cocoa

⅔ cup sugar

4 egg whites

½ cup plain low-fat yogurt

1 tablespoon baking powder

½ teaspoon baking soda

¼ teaspoon salt

1 teaspoon vanilla

½ teaspoon xanthan gum

1. Preheat oven to 350°F.

2. Mix flour and oil until well combined.

3. Add remaining ingredients. Beat until well blended.

4. Pour into a lightly greased 8-inch round pan.

5. Bake 20–25 minutes, until a toothpick inserted in the middle tests clean, and cake is lightly browned on top.

Eggnog Pound Cake

– Brown Rice Flour –
SERVES 9

I recall being at a conference and discussing my two theories for making a favorite cake recipe gluten-free. My hypothetical example was grandma's Eggnog Pound Cake. (I've included those theories on page 199.) Finally, I decided that the hypothetical example sounded so good, I had to make it a real recipe! And it is really good!

¼ cup canola oil

¾ cup brown rice flour, 95 grams

½ cup sugar

3 eggs

⅓ cup eggnog

2 teaspoons baking powder

¼ teaspoon baking soda

¼ teaspoon salt

¾ teaspoon xanthan gum

¼ teaspoon nutmeg

ICING:

½ cup confectioners' sugar

1 tablespoon eggnog

Pinch of nutmeg (optional)

1. Preheat oven to 350°F.
2. Mix flour and oil until well combined.
3. Add remaining ingredients. Beat until well blended.
4. Pour into a lightly greased 8 x 4-inch loaf pan.
5. Bake 30–40 minutes, until a toothpick inserted in the middle tests clean, and cake is lightly browned on top.

Peanut Butter Cake

– Brown Rice Flour –
SERVES 2

I love chocolate cake with peanut butter icing. That made me wonder what would happen if I made peanut butter cake with chocolate icing? Even better, you can bake this in the microwave— a decadent treat in about 5 minutes!

1 egg

3 tablespoons peanut butter

3 tablespoons applesauce

1/16 teaspoon (pinch) salt

1 1/2 tablespoons brown rice flour

1/2 teaspoon baking powder

1 1/2 tablespoons sugar

1/4 teaspoon vanilla

1. In a small bowl or cup, briefly beat egg until almost uniform in color.

2. Add remaining ingredients, and mix well to combine.

3. Spray a 2-cup ramekin or straight-sided baking dish with nonstick cooking spray.

4. Pour batter into dish, and tap base to level batter.

5. Microwave on high for 2 minutes. Cake will rise and then settle a little during baking.

6. Gently remove from dish and cool.

7. Ice as desired.

Pumpkin Spice Cake

– Sorghum Flour –
SERVES 9

◆

Move over carrot cake! You have some competition!
With a little cream cheese icing, this could be a new family favorite.
It is lightly spiced, quite moist, not light, but not heavy in texture.
Having a can of plain pumpkin in your pantry can lead to a great dessert.

¼ cup canola oil

¾ cup sorghum flour, 95 grams

½ cup sugar

2 eggs

½ cup pumpkin (canned)

1 tablespoon baking powder

1 teaspoon baking soda

¼ teaspoon salt

½ teaspoon cinnamon

¼ teaspoon nutmeg

½ teaspoon apple cider vinegar

½ teaspoon xanthan gum

¼ cup finely chopped nuts (optional)

¼ cup finely chopped raisins (optional)

1. Preheat oven to 350°F.
2. Mix flour and oil until well combined.
3. Add remaining ingredients, except nuts and raisins. Beat until well blended.
4. Add nuts and raisins, if using.
5. Pour into a lightly greased 8- or 9-inch round or square pan.
6. Bake 20–25 minutes, until a toothpick inserted in the middle tests clean, and cake is lightly browned on top.

Red Velvet Cupcakes

– White Rice Flour –
SERVES 10

*When I saw beautiful red velvet cupcakes in my local market,
I knew I had to create a gluten-free version for you. I used white rice flour
for a more delicate crumb, just as you'd find in a red velvet cake. You can
substitute brown rice flour; just expect a slightly heavier crumb.*

¼ cup canola oil

¾ cup white rice flour minus 1 tablespoon, 105 grams

1½ tablespoons cocoa

½ cup sugar

1 egg plus 2 egg whites

½ cup plain low-fat yogurt

1 tablespoon baking powder

¼ teaspoon salt

1 teaspoon vanilla

½ teaspoon xanthan gum

1 teaspoon red food coloring

1 teaspoon baking soda

1 teaspoon apple cider vinegar

1. Preheat oven to 350°F.
2. Mix flour and oil until well combined.
3. Add remaining ingredients, except baking soda and vinegar. Beat until well blended.
4. Put baking soda in a small cup. Add vinegar. Stir quickly, and then pour over batter.
5. Fold in as quickly as possible.
6. Pour into 10 cupcake liners.
7. Bake 15–18 minutes, until a toothpick inserted in the middle of one tests clean, and cupcakes are lightly browned on top.

Soft Chocolate Cake

– Brown Rice Flour –
SERVES 9

❖

This soft, squishy cake is flat-topped and quite moist. Brown rice provides a wonderful neutral backdrop for the chocolate flavor.

¼ cup canola oil

¾ cup minus 1 tablespoon brown rice flour, 90 grams

¼ cup cocoa

½ cup sugar

2 eggs plus 1 egg white

½ cup plain low-fat yogurt

1 tablespoon baking powder

½ teaspoon baking soda

¼ teaspoon salt

1 teaspoon vanilla

½ teaspoon xanthan gum

1. Preheat oven to 350°F.

2. Mix flour and oil until well combined.

3. Add remaining ingredients. Beat until well blended.

4. Pour into a lightly greased 8- or 9-inch round or square pan.

5. Bake 20–25 minutes, until a toothpick inserted in the middle tests clean, and cake is lightly browned on top.

Soft Chocolate Cake

– Sorghum Flour –
SERVES 9

✦

This is a flat-topped, everyday chocolate cake. It will bake better in an 8-inch pan. Because chocolate has such a robust flavor, it pairs well with sorghum flour.

¼ cup canola oil

½ cup plus 2 tablespoons sorghum flour, 65 grams

¼ cup cocoa (dark chocolate preferred)

½ cup sugar

2 eggs

½ cup plain low-fat yogurt

1 tablespoon baking powder

½ teaspoon baking soda

¼ teaspoon salt

1 teaspoon vanilla

½ teaspoon xanthan gum

1. Preheat oven to 350°F.

2. Mix flour and oil until well combined.

3. Add remaining ingredients. Beat until well blended.

4. Pour into a lightly greased 8-inch round or square pan.

5. Bake 20–25 minutes, until a toothpick inserted in the middle tests clean, and cake is lightly browned on top.

You Still Won't Believe It's Gluten-Free

210

Soft Yellow Cake

– Brown Rice Flour –
SERVES 9

*This is a simple, soft yellow cake, just like
you enjoyed before going gluten-free.*

¼ cup canola oil

¾ cup brown rice flour,
100 grams

½ cup sugar

2 eggs

½ cup plain low-fat yogurt

1 tablespoon baking powder

1 teaspoon baking soda

¼ teaspoon salt

1 teaspoon vanilla

½ teaspoon xanthan gum

1. Preheat oven to 350°F.

2. Mix flour and oil until well
combined.

3. Add remaining ingredients. Beat
until well blended.

4. Pour into a lightly greased 8- or
9-inch round or square pan.

5. Bake 20–25 minutes, until a toothpick inserted in the middle tests
clean, and cake is lightly browned
on top.

Cakes

Vanilla Pound Cake

– Brown Rice Flour –
SERVES 9

This is a pound cake like you remember, if you ever had a "from-scratch" pound cake before eating gluten-free. It is not overly sweet, has a bit of weight, and yet remains moist and tender.

¼ cup canola oil

¾ cup brown rice flour, 95 grams

½ cup sugar

3 eggs

⅓ cup plain low-fat yogurt

2 teaspoons baking powder

¼ teaspoon baking soda

¼ teaspoon salt

¾ teaspoon xanthan gum

1½ teaspoons vanilla

1. Preheat oven to 350°F.

2. Mix flour and oil until well combined.

3. Add remaining ingredients. Beat until well blended.

4. Pour into a lightly greased 8 x 4-inch loaf pan.

5. Bake 30–40 minutes, until a toothpick inserted in the middle tests clean, and cake is lightly browned on top.

White Cake—8-inch layer

– White Rice Flour –
SERVES 9

◆

Not so long ago, a light and not overly squishy cake made with just rice flour would have been thought impossible. Not so any longer! This cake rises nicely and has a delicate, understated flavor. If you want a stronger flavor, add a little extra vanilla. It is really good. This easy cake would be lovely for a wedding cake.

¼ cup canola oil

¾ cup white rice flour,
115 grams

½ cup sugar

4 egg whites

½ cup plain low-fat yogurt

1 tablespoon baking powder

1 teaspoon baking soda

¼ teaspoon salt

1 teaspoon vanilla

½ teaspoon xanthan gum

1. Preheat oven to 350°F.

2. Mix flour and oil until well combined.

3. Add remaining ingredients. Beat until well blended.

4. Pour into a lightly greased 8-inch round or square pan.

5. Bake 20–25 minutes, until a toothpick inserted in the middle tests clean, and cake is lightly browned on top.

Yellow Cake—8-inch layer

¼ cup canola oil

¾ cup white rice flour,
115 grams

½ cup sugar

2 eggs

½ cup plain low-fat yogurt

1 tablespoon baking powder

1 teaspoon baking soda

¼ teaspoon salt

1 teaspoon vanilla

½ teaspoon xanthan gum

½ teaspoon apple cider vinegar

1. Preheat oven to 350°F.

2. Mix flour and oil until well combined.

3. Add remaining ingredients. Beat until well blended.

4. Pour into a lightly greased 8-inch round or square pan.

5. Bake 20–25 minutes, until a toothpick inserted in the middle tests clean, and cake is lightly browned on top.

CHAPTER 14

Special Cake Layers

This **chapter has** three distinct types of cake layers: white, chocolate, and yellow. Although they are ideal for any special occasion, they are often called wedding cake layers.

The white cake layers are amazing. They have wonderful moisture retention. Their texture is somewhat like a cross between an angel food cake and a pound cake. If I were needing white wedding cake layers, I would choose these—gluten-free or not. These layers bake quite high and settle slightly. I use Wilton's standard 1½-inch baking pans; shorter pans should be avoided. These layers are nearly flat, with a firm, crumb-free exterior. And, with a light spraying of the pans with nonstick spray, the layers come away quite easily from the pan.

As for flavor, these layers are not too sweet. I believe this a good approach given the sweetness of icing. This cake tastes softly of vanilla, but it is by no means strong. If you desire an alternative flavoring, I would use butter or almond extract of equal amounts.

The texture of the chocolate cake layers is perfect, not too heavy and not too light. They are soft without being squishy, almost firm. They bake into tall, very flat layers, with a firm, crumb-free exterior. I use standard Wilton baking pans to ensure sufficient baking room. And, with a light spraying of the pans with nonstick spray, the layers come away quite easily from the pan.

And, like the white cake layers, these layers are not too sweet. Try them with one of the icings in Chapter 15. This cake tastes quite chocolatey, but the flavor is not overwhelming.

The yellow cake layers are perhaps the most delicate in this chapter. They are the softest and springiest of the bunch. They bake into very flat layers, with a firm, crumb-free exterior. And with a light spraying of the pans with nonstick spray, the layers come away quite easily from the pan.

As with the other two flavors, these layers are not too sweet. I leave that for the icing. This cake tastes like a yellow cake, not a vanilla cake. This cake also makes a nice lemon cake. Should you want the flavor of vanilla (or lemon) to be more pronounced, increase the extract measure by half.

Chocolate Cake—6-inch layer

2 tablespoons canola oil

⅓ cup white rice flour,
   50 grams

2 tablespoons cocoa

⅓ cup sugar

2 egg whites

¼ cup plain low-fat yogurt

1½ teaspoons baking powder

¼ teaspoon baking soda

⅛ teaspoon salt

½ teaspoon vanilla

¼ teaspoon xanthan gum

1. Preheat oven to 350°F.
2. Mix flour and oil until well combined.
3. Add remaining ingredients. Beat until well blended.
4. Pour into a lightly greased 6-inch round pan.
5. Bake 20–25 minutes, until a toothpick inserted in the middle tests clean, and the cake is lightly browned on top.

Chocolate Cake—8-inch layer

– White Rice Flour –
SERVES 9

This chocolate cake is delicate in taste and texture but easy in form and would be lovely for a wedding cake. Be careful in measuring the rising agents as too much will cause the cake to sink. (Although contrary to what seems to make sense at first, it is absolutely true!)

¼ cup canola oil

⅔ cup white rice flour, 100 grams

¼ cup cocoa

⅔ cup sugar

4 egg whites

½ cup plain low-fat yogurt

1 tablespoon baking powder

½ teaspoon baking soda

¼ teaspoon salt

1 teaspoon vanilla

½ teaspoon xanthan gum

1. Preheat oven to 350°F.

2. Mix flour and oil until well combined.

3. Add remaining ingredients. Beat until well blended.

4. Pour into a lightly greased 8-inch round pan.

5. Bake 20–25 minutes, until a toothpick inserted in the middle tests clean, and cake is lightly browned on top.

Chocolate Cake—10-inch layer

– White Rice Flour –
SERVES 9

⬧

1/3 cup canola oil

1 cup white rice flour,
150 grams

1/3 cup cocoa

1 cup sugar

6 egg whites

3/4 cup plain low-fat yogurt

1 1/2 tablespoons baking powder

3/4 teaspoon baking soda

Scant 1/2 teaspoon salt

1 1/2 teaspoons vanilla

3/4 teaspoon xanthan gum

1. Preheat oven to 350°F.

2. Mix flour and oil until well combined.

3. Add remaining ingredients. Beat until well blended.

4. Pour into a lightly greased 10-inch round pan.

5. Bake 20–25 minutes, until a toothpick inserted in the middle tests clean, and cake is lightly browned on top.

Chocolate Cake—12-inch layer

½ cup canola oil

1⅓ cups white rice flour, 200 grams

½ cup cocoa

1⅓ cups sugar

8 egg whites

1 cup plain low-fat yogurt

2 tablespoons baking powder

1 teaspoon baking soda

½ teaspoon salt

2 teaspoons vanilla

1 teaspoon xanthan gum

1. Preheat oven to 350°F.
2. Mix flour and oil until well combined.
3. Add remaining ingredients. Beat until well blended.
4. Pour into a lightly greased 12-inch round pan.
5. Bake 20–25 minutes, until a toothpick inserted in the middle tests clean, and cake is lightly browned on top.

White Cake—6-Inch Layer

– White Rice Flour –
SERVES 9

This cake rises nicely and has a delicate, understated flavor.
If you want a stronger flavor, add a little extra vanilla. It is just good.
This easy cake would be lovely for a wedding cake.

2 tablespoons canola oil

1/3 cup plus 1 tablespoon white rice flour, 60 grams

1/4 cup sugar

2 egg whites

1/4 cup plain low-fat yogurt

1 1/2 teaspoons baking powder

1/2 teaspoon baking soda

1/8 teaspoon salt

1/2 teaspoon vanilla

1/4 teaspoon xanthan gum

1. Preheat oven to 350°F.

2. Mix flour and oil until well combined.

3. Add remaining ingredients. Beat until well blended.

4. Pour into a lightly greased 6-inch round pan.

5. Bake approximately 20 minutes, until a toothpick inserted in the middle tests clean, and cake is lightly browned on top.

White Cake—8-inch layer

¼ cup canola oil

¾ cup white rice flour, 115 grams

½ cup sugar

4 egg whites

½ cup plain low-fat yogurt

1 tablespoon baking powder

1 teaspoon baking soda

¼ teaspoon salt

1 teaspoon vanilla

½ teaspoon xanthan gum

1. Preheat oven to 350°F.

2. Mix flour and oil until well combined.

3. Add remaining ingredients. Beat until well blended.

4. Pour into a lightly greased 8-inch round pan.

5. Bake 20–25 minutes, until a toothpick inserted in the middle tests clean, and cake is lightly browned on top.

White Cake—10-Inch Layer

– White Rice Flour –
SERVES 9

◀▸

⅓ cup canola oil

1 cup plus 2 tablespoons white rice flour, 170 grams

¾ cup sugar

6 egg whites

¾ cup plain low-fat yogurt

1½ tablespoons baking powder

1½ teaspoons baking soda

Scant ½ teaspoon salt

1½ teaspoons vanilla

¾ teaspoon xanthan gum

1. Preheat oven to 350°F.
2. Mix flour and oil until well combined.
3. Add remaining ingredients. Beat until well blended.
4. Pour into a lightly greased 10-inch round pan.
5. Bake 25–30 minutes, until a toothpick inserted in the middle tests clean, and cake is lightly browned on top.

White Cake—12-inch layer

– White Rice Flour –
SERVES 9

½ cup canola oil

1½ cups white rice flour, 230 grams

1 cup sugar

8 egg whites

1 cup plain low-fat yogurt

2 tablespoons baking powder

2 teaspoons baking soda

½ teaspoon salt

2 teaspoons vanilla

1 teaspoon xanthan gum

1. Preheat oven to 350°F.

2. Mix flour and oil until well combined.

3. Add remaining ingredients. Beat until well blended.

4. Pour into a lightly greased 12-inch round pan.

5. Bake 20–25 minutes, until a toothpick inserted in the middle tests clean, and cake is lightly browned on top.

Yellow Cake—6-Inch Layer

– White Rice Flour –
SERVES 9

2 tablespoons canola oil

⅓ cup plus 1 tablespoon white rice flour, 60 grams

¼ cup sugar

1 egg

¼ cup plain low-fat yogurt

1½ teaspoons baking powder

½ teaspoon baking soda

⅛ teaspoon salt

½ teaspoon vanilla

¼ teaspoon xanthan gum

¼ teaspoon apple cider vinegar

1. Preheat oven to 350°F.

2. Mix flour and oil until well combined.

3. Add remaining ingredients. Beat until well blended.

4. Pour into a lightly greased 6-inch round pan.

5. Bake approximately 20 minutes, until a toothpick inserted in the middle tests clean, and cake is lightly browned on top.

Yellow Cake—8-inch layer

– White Rice Flour –
SERVES 9

¼ cup canola oil

¾ cup white rice flour,
115 grams

½ cup sugar

2 eggs

½ cup plain low-fat yogurt

1 tablespoon baking powder

1 teaspoon baking soda

¼ teaspoon salt

1 teaspoon vanilla

½ teaspoon xanthan gum

½ teaspoon apple cider vinegar

1. Preheat oven to 350°F.

2. Mix flour and oil until well combined.

3. Add remaining ingredients. Beat until well blended.

4. Pour into a lightly greased 8-inch round pan.

5. Bake 20–25 minutes, until a toothpick inserted in the middle tests clean, and cake is lightly browned on top.

Yellow Cake—10-Inch Layer

– White Rice Flour –
SERVES 9

❖

⅓ cup canola oil

1 cup plus 2 tablespoons white rice flour, 170 grams

¾ cup sugar

3 eggs

¾ cup plain low-fat yogurt

1½ tablespoons baking powder

1½ teaspoons baking soda

Scant ½ teaspoon salt

1½ teaspoons vanilla

¾ teaspoon xanthan gum

¾ teaspoon apple cider vinegar

1. Preheat oven to 350°F.

2. Mix flour and oil until well combined.

3. Add remaining ingredients. Beat until well blended.

4. Pour into a lightly greased 10-inch round pan.

5. Bake 25–30 minutes, until a toothpick inserted in the middle tests clean, and cake is lightly browned on top.

Yellow Cake—12-inch layer

– White Rice Flour –
SERVES 9

½ cup canola oil

1½ cups white rice flour, 230 grams

1 cup sugar

4 eggs

1 cup plain low-fat yogurt

2 tablespoons baking powder

2 teaspoons baking soda

½ teaspoon salt

2 teaspoons vanilla

1 teaspoon xanthan gum

1 teaspoon apple cider vinegar

1. Preheat oven to 350°F.

2. Mix flour and oil until well combined.

3. Add remaining ingredients. Beat until well blended.

4. Pour into a lightly greased 12-inch round pan.

5. Bake 20–25 minutes, until a tooth-pick inserted in the middle tests clean, and cake is lightly browned on top.

CHAPTER 15

Icings and Other Toppings

◀◆▶

For this chapter to be complete, I had to "borrow" a few of my favorite icing recipes from *You Won't Believe It's Gluten-Free*. But don't worry, I've also created some new recipes just for you.

Here you'll find soft versions of royal icing—that stiff, super-sweet icing often used on wedding cakes. With a few little modifications, this "overly sweet" icing has been transformed into variations that are creamy, soft, and spread like a dream. It's amazing what a little xanthan gum and a little extra liquid will do to an icing! Although I didn't know it at the time I "discovered" this secret, it is a common trick of the pros!

And for the purist, I've included a Cream Cheese Icing, too.

Chocolate Whipped Cream

SERVES 8

◆

This is a super-stable chocolate whipped cream.
Seriously, what could possibly be better? Slice a pound cake horizontally,
grab some fresh raspberries, a little jam, and layer away!

1 cup heavy cream

¼ cup confectioners' sugar

½ teaspoon vanilla

⅛ teaspoon xanthan gum

1 square chocolate,
 melted and cooled

1. In a medium bowl, combine cream, about half the confectioners' sugar, and vanilla. Beat to almost soft peaks.

2. Beat in melted chocolate.

3. Mix xanthan gum and remaining confectioners' sugar in a small cup.

4. Sprinkle over cream. Beat to soft peaks.

Note: Isn't it interesting that the chocolate version of whipped cream requires more sugar?

Cream Cheese Icing

MAKES ABOUT 2 CUPS

◆

This is the classic icing for carrot cake.
Try this on chocolate cake, too!

8 ounces cream cheese

1 pound confectioners' sugar

1 teaspoon vanilla

3 tablespoons milk

1. In a medium bowl, combine all ingredients, except milk.

2. Slowly blend with a mixer, adding milk slowly. Do not use more milk than necessary.

3. Beat until soft and creamy. Continue beating for an additional 2–3 minutes to lose the "raw" sugar taste.

Creamy Chocolate Royal Icing

MAKES ABOUT 3 CUPS

◆

This creamy icing may seem to have a strong chocolate flavor straight from the bowl. However, it nicely balances the sweetness of a cake when it's spread. Also, it may seem like you would need less liquid in the recipe, given the addition of melted chocolate, but that's not the case. If anything, this icing is a bit stiffer than my original Creamy Royal Icing.

½ cup shortening

1 pound confectioners' sugar

1 teaspoon vanilla

¼ teaspoon xanthan gum

⅓ cup water

2 squares unsweetened chocolate, melted and cooled

1. In a medium bowl, combine all ingredients, except water and chocolate.

2. Slowly blend with a mixer, adding water slowly. Beat until soft and creamy.

3. Pour cooled, melted chocolate over the icing, and continue beating for an additional 2–3 minutes to lose the "raw" sugar taste.

Note: To melt chocolate, place chocolate in a microwave-safe cup or bowl. Microwave on high for 60–80 seconds, checking chocolate at 20-second intervals to be sure it doesn't melt faster than expected. Stir and allow to cool.

Creamy Royal Icing

MAKES ABOUT 3 CUPS

This just may be the perfect wedding cake icing. It is a dream to spread! It is also lighter and seems less sweet than traditional royal icing.

½ cup shortening

1 pound confectioners' sugar

1 teaspoon vanilla

¼ teaspoon xanthan gum

⅓ cup water

1. In a medium bowl, combine all ingredients, except water.
2. Slowly blend with a mixer, adding water slowly. Beat until soft and creamy.
3. Continue beating for an additional 2–3 minutes to lose the "raw" sugar taste.

Icings and Other Toppings

Creamy Tangy Royal Icing

MAKES ABOUT 2½ CUPS

◆

This icing is light and delicate, with a bit of twang, reminiscent of cream cheese icing. If you want to pipe it, reduce the amount of yogurt just a bit.

½ cup shortening

1 pound confectioners' sugar

¾ teaspoon vanilla

¼ teaspoon xanthan gum

⅓ cup plain low-fat yogurt

1. In a medium bowl, combine all ingredients, except yogurt.

2. Slowly blend with a mixer, adding yogurt slowly. Beat until soft and creamy.

3. Continue beating for an additional 2–3 minutes to lose the "raw" sugar taste.

Velvet Icing—Brown Sugar

– Cornstarch, Potato Starch –

By using brown sugar in this recipe, we achieve a bit of toffee flavor!

FOR TWO 8- OR 9-INCH CAKE LAYERS:

1 cup milk

2½ tablespoons cornstarch or potato starch

1 cup butter

1 cup brown sugar

1 teaspoon vanilla

FOR SINGLE 8- OR 9-INCH CAKE LAYER:

½ cup milk

1 tablespoon plus ¾ teaspoon cornstarch or potato starch

½ cup butter

½ cup brown sugar

½ teaspoon vanilla

1. In a microwave-safe bowl, combine milk and cornstarch. Stir well.

2. Microwave this mixture on high for 2–4 minutes, until quite thick. Stir periodically to better incorporate ingredients. These ingredients may also be cooked in a saucepan over medium heat. Stir constantly if using this method.

3. Cover thickened milk mixture with plastic wrap touching its surface. Or spray surface with nonstick spray. Either approach will help prevent "skin" from forming. Cool to room temperature. If skin forms, you can discard it later.

4. In a medium bowl, cream butter, sugar, and vanilla. Mix until light and fluffy.

5. Add milk mixture (with skin removed, if necessary), and beat until frosting looks like whipped cream. This will take several minutes.

Icings and Other Toppings

Velvet Icing—Vanilla

– Cornstarch, Potato Starch –

Homemade cake is better with homemade frosting. Once you have mastered this recipe, I'm sure it will become a family favorite. My grandmother was the original source of this lovely recipe. She served it on red velvet cake.

FOR TWO 8- OR 9-INCH CAKE LAYERS:

1 cup milk

2½ tablespoons cornstarch or potato starch

1 cup butter

1 cup sugar

2 teaspoons vanilla

FOR SINGLE 8- OR 9-INCH CAKE LAYER:

½ cup milk

1 tablespoon plus ¾ teaspoon cornstarch or potato starch

½ cup butter

½ cup sugar

1 teaspoon vanilla

1. In a microwave-safe bowl, combine milk and cornstarch. Stir well. Microwave this mixture on high for 2–4 minutes, until quite thick. Stir periodically to better incorporate ingredients. These ingredients may also be cooked in a saucepan over medium heat. Stir constantly if using this method.

2. Cover thickened milk mixture with plastic wrap touching its surface. Or spray surface with nonstick spray. Either approach will help prevent "skin" from forming. Cool to room temperature. If skin forms, you can discard it later.

3. In a medium bowl, cream butter, sugar, and vanilla. Mix until light and fluffy. Add milk mixture (with skin removed, if necessary), and beat until frosting looks like whipped cream. This will take several minutes.

Whipped Cream

SERVES 8

⬥

The stability of this whipped cream comes from just a little bit of xanthan gum. This whipped cream easily holds for a week in the refrigerator. It would be beautiful piped on cakes, pies, ice cream, or even into some delicious coffee!

1 cup heavy cream

2 tablespoons confectioners' sugar

2 teaspoons vanilla liqueur or ½ teaspoon vanilla

⅛ teaspoon xanthan gum

1. In a medium bowl, combine cream, 1 tablespoon confectioners' sugar, and vanilla liqueur. Beat to almost soft peaks.

2. Mix xanthan gum and remaining 1 tablespoon confectioners' sugar in a small cup. Sprinkle over cream. Beat to soft peaks.

Note: Use of a distilled vanilla liqueur (not flavored) extends the flavor, giving a longer mellow vanilla taste than just vanilla flavoring. A fine vanilla extract is often based in bourbon, which would also provide a better flavor.

For an incredible variation, omit the vanilla liqueur or vanilla and add 1 tablespoon of seedless jam. Black raspberry is very good.

Icings and Other Toppings

CHAPTER 16

Cookies and Bars

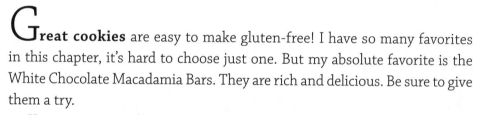

Great cookies are easy to make gluten-free! I have so many favorites in this chapter, it's hard to choose just one. But my absolute favorite is the White Chocolate Macadamia Bars. They are rich and delicious. Be sure to give them a try.

You may notice that I've kept the quantity of cookies made with each recipe rather small, as fresh cookies are always better. If you decide to freeze extras, place a piece of waxed paper between the cookies to prevent their sticking to each other.

For a wider variety of cookies, please check out my *Ultimate Gluten-Free Cookie Book*. I've included two favorites from that book here as well—the Rolled Sugar Cookies, Dairy Free, and Peanut Butter Blossom Cookies.

Brownies

These brownies have a cake-like texture with a bit of "chew" and that traditional crispy edge. They are not overly sweet. Nuts are optional, but chopped peanuts, walnuts, or almonds make a nice addition.

¼ cup butter

½ cup sorghum flour, 65 grams

¼ cup cocoa

¾ cup brown sugar

2 eggs

¼ teaspoon baking soda

¼ teaspoon salt

½ teaspoon xanthan gum

1 teaspoon vanilla

½ cup chopped nuts (optional)

1. Preheat oven to 350°F.

2. Mix flour and butter until well combined.

3. Add remaining ingredients, except nuts.

4. Beat batter until well combined and thickened. This will help prevent nuts from sinking.

5. Fold in nuts. Pour into 9-inch square baking pan.

6. Bake 15–25 minutes, until edges begin to pull away and bars test clean with a toothpick.

7. Cut into 12 large bars.

Chocolate Chip Cookies

– Brown Rice Flour –
MAKES ABOUT 25 COOKIES

I know, I know. Every cookbook has chocolate chip cookies.
How can it not? I think you will rank these among your favorites.

¼ cup butter

¾ cup brown rice flour,
   95 grams

½ cup brown sugar

2 eggs

¼ teaspoon baking soda

¼ teaspoon salt

1 teaspoon vanilla

½ teaspoon xanthan gum

¾ cup chocolate chips

1. Preheat oven to 350°F.

2. Mix flour and butter until well combined.

3. Add remaining ingredients, except chips.

4. Beat batter well, until batter is quite thick.

5. Stir in chips.

6. Drop by rounded teaspoonful onto lightly greased baking sheet.

7. Press tops with moist fingertips to flatten just a little.

8. Bake 10–12 minutes, until edges are lightly browned, and cookies are set.

9. Cool on wire racks.

Cookies and Bars

241

Chocolate Chip Cookies

– Sorghum Flour –
MAKES ABOUT 25 COOKIES

*Here's a buttery version of the classic cookie.
They really are awfully good!*

¼ cup butter

¾ cup sorghum flour,
  100 grams

½ cup brown sugar

1 egg plus 1 egg white

¼ teaspoon baking soda

¼ teaspoon salt

¾ teaspoon xanthan gum

1 teaspoon vanilla

½ cup chocolate chips

1. Preheat oven to 350°F.
2. Mix flour and butter until well combined.
3. Add remaining ingredients, except chips.
4. Beat well until batter is quite thick.
5. Stir in chips.
6. Drop by rounded teaspoonful onto lightly greased baking sheet.
7. Press tops with moist fingertips to flatten just a little.
8. Bake 9–10 minutes, until edges are lightly browned, and cookies are set.
9. Cool on wire racks.

Note: If cookies seem a little poofy, that means that you beat the batter longer than I did during testing, and the xanthan gum gave more structure to the dough. Just press the tops down with moist fingertips before baking.

Chocolate Cookies

– Sorghum Flour –
MAKES ABOUT 25 COOKIES

✦

These cookies are dusted with confectioners' sugar before baking, making for a pretty and delicious cookie! They're soft, not too sweet, and chocolatey.

¼ cup butter

½ cup sorghum flour,
   65 grams

¼ cup cocoa

½ cup brown sugar

1 egg plus 1 egg white

¼ teaspoon baking soda

¼ teaspoon salt

¾ teaspoon xanthan gum

1 teaspoon vanilla

TOPPING:

2 tablespoons confectioners'
   sugar

1. Preheat oven to 350°F.
2. Mix flour, cocoa, and butter until well combined.
3. Add remaining ingredients.
4. Beat well until batter is quite thick.
5. Drop by rounded teaspoonful onto lightly greased baking sheet.
6. Press tops with moist fingertips to flatten just a little.
7. Sift confectioners' sugar on the tops to coat well.
8. Bake 9–10 minutes, until edges are lightly browned, and cookies are set.
9. Cool on wire racks.

Ginger Cookies with Icing

– Sorghum Flour –
MAKES ABOUT 25 COOKIES

*Ginger cookies from our wonderful little bakery here in town,
called Icings, were the inspiration for these cookies.*

¼ cup butter

¾ cup sorghum flour,
  100 grams

½ cup dark brown sugar

1 egg plus 1 egg white

¼ teaspoon baking soda

¼ teaspoon salt

¾ teaspoon xanthan gum

2 teaspoons ground ginger

¼ teaspoon vanilla

ICING:

½ cup confectioners' sugar

1 teaspoon vanilla

1 teaspoon water

1. Preheat oven to 350°F.

2. Mix flour and butter until well combined.

3. Add remaining ingredients. Beat well until batter is quite thick.

4. Drop by rounded teaspoonful onto lightly greased baking sheet.

5. Press tops with moist fingertips to flatten just a little.

6. Bake 9–10 minutes, until edges are lightly browned, and cookies are set.

7. Cool on wire racks.

8. For icing, mix confectioners' sugar, vanilla and water. Pour icing into a puddle in the middle of the cookie tops, and let it run down the sides. Or, just drizzle it over the tops.

Oatmeal Raisin Spice Cookies

– Brown Rice Flour, Oatmeal –
MAKES ABOUT 25 COOKIES

These are soft, tender cookies with oats and raisins.
Please make sure you buy safe, gluten-free oats.
Then enjoy! The nutmeg provides a nice "bite" of flavor.

¼ cup butter

¾ cup brown rice flour,
  95 grams

½ cup sugar

1 egg plus 1 egg white

¼ teaspoon baking soda

¼ teaspoon salt

¼ teaspoon cinnamon

⅛ teaspoon nutmeg

½ cup quick oats

½ teaspoon xanthan gum

½ cup raisins

1. Preheat oven to 350°F.
2. Mix flour and butter until well combined.
3. Add remaining ingredients, except raisins.
4. Beat well until batter is quite thick.
5. Stir in raisins.
6. Drop by rounded teaspoonful onto lightly greased baking sheet.
7. Press tops with moist fingertips to flatten just a little.
8. Bake 10–12 minutes, until edges are lightly browned, and cookies are set.
9. Cool on wire racks.

Peanut Butter Blossom Cookies

– Brown Rice Flour, Cornstarch –
MAKES ABOUT 26 COOKIES

This is a classic peanut butter cookie with a milk chocolate kiss right in the middle. The cookie has a light tenderness to it that blends perfectly with the milk chocolate flavor.

¼ cup creamy peanut butter

2 tablespoons canola oil

½ cup brown sugar

1 cup brown rice flour, 125 grams

⅓ cup cornstarch, 40 grams

1 egg

¼ teaspoon baking soda

1 teaspoon baking powder

½ teaspoon salt

1 teaspoon xanthan gum

1 teaspoon vanilla

2 tablespoons water

TOPPING:

1 to 2 tablespoons sugar

26 milk chocolate kisses

1. Preheat the oven to 350°F.

2. Lightly grease a cookie sheet.

3. In a medium-sized bowl, combine the peanut butter, oil, and sugar. Beat well. Add the brown rice flour and cornstarch, and beat well. Scrape down the sides of the mixing bowl at least once during mixing. Add the remaining ingredients, and beat well. Continue beating until the dough comes together.

4. Shape the dough into 1-inch balls. Roll them in sugar, and place them on the prepared pan. Press the tops to flatten them slightly.

5. Bake the cookies for 10–12 minutes, until the edges begin to have a hint of browning.

6. Remove the sheet from the oven. Immediately press an unwrapped chocolate kiss into the center of each cookie.

7. Cool on wire racks before serving.

Pumpkin Cookies

– Sorghum Flour –
MAKES ABOUT 25 COOKIES

❖

These cookies are lightly spiced and soft. For variety, try using ½ cup
mini chocolate chips, and omit the pumpkin pie spice and icing.

¼ cup butter

¾ cup sorghum flour,
   100 grams

½ cup sugar

1 egg plus 1 egg white

¼ teaspoon baking soda

¼ teaspoon salt

¾ teaspoon xanthan gum

1 teaspoon pumpkin pie spice

½ teaspoon vanilla

ICING (OPTIONAL):

½ cup confectioners' sugar

¼ teaspoon vanilla

2 teaspoons milk

1. Preheat oven to 350°F.

2. Mix flour and butter until well combined.

3. Add remaining ingredients.

4. Beat well until batter is quite thick.

5. Drop by rounded teaspoonful onto lightly greased baking sheet.

6. Press tops with moist fingertips to flatten just a little.

7. Bake 9–10 minutes, until edges are lightly browned, and cookies are set.

8. Cool on wire racks.

9. For icing, mix confectioners' sugar, vanilla, and milk. Drizzle over the tops of the cookies.

Rolled Cream Cheese Sugar Cookies

– Brown Rice Flour –
MAKES ABOUT 25 COOKIES OR 4 4-INCH TART CRUSTS

This is a soft sugar cookie dough that can be rolled out after just 30 minutes in the freezer. This cookie dough forms the crust for my tart recipes as well.

½ cup cream cheese

¾ cup brown rice flour,
  95 grams

½ cup sugar

1 egg

¼ teaspoon baking soda

¼ teaspoon salt

½ teaspoon xanthan gum

1 teaspoon vanilla

1. Preheat oven to 350°F.

2. Mix flour and cream cheese until well combined.

3. Add remaining ingredients. Beat well. Batter will be thick and tacky.

4. Place dough in the freezer for 30 minutes before rolling out.

5. Roll to ¼-inch thick, and cut out cookies with cookie or biscuit cutter. Place onto lightly greased baking sheet. Or drop by rounded teaspoon onto lightly greased baking sheet.

6. Press tops with moist fingertips to flatten just a little.

7. Bake 10–12 minutes, until edges are lightly browned, and cookies are set.

8. Cool on wire racks.

Rolled Sugar Cookies, Dairy-Free

– Brown Rice Flour –
MAKES ABOUT 30 COOKIES

Here is a dairy-free version of a rolled sugar cookie.
They are simply delicious.

⅓ cup shortening

½ cup sugar

1½ cups brown rice flour,
   185 grams

1 egg

1½ teaspoons baking powder

½ teaspoon salt

1 teaspoon xanthan gum

1 teaspoon vanilla

1½ teaspoons water

TOPPING (OPTIONAL):

Sprinkles or colored sugar

1. Preheat the oven to 350°F.

2. Lightly grease a baking sheet.

3. In a medium-sized bowl, combine the shortening and sugar. Beat well. Add the flour and beat well. Scrape down the sides of the mixing bowl at least once during mixing. Add the remaining ingredients and mix well.

4. The cookie dough will form large clumps, but it will not quite come together to form a ball. Press it together with your hands.

5. Roll out the dough to ¼ inch, and cut it with a 2-inch round cookie cutter (or other cookie cutter of your choice).

6. Place the cookies on the prepared pan. Top with sprinkles or colored sugar, if desired.

7. Bake the cookies for 8–10 minutes, until they have the slightest hint of color, and the tops are dry.

8. Cool on wire racks.

Cookies and Bars

Snickerdoodles

– Brown Rice Flour –
MAKES ABOUT 25 COOKIES

This is another of my favorites. For sugar cookies, just roll in plain sugar instead of the cinnamon-sugar mixture.

¼ cup butter

¾ cup brown rice flour, 95 grams

½ cup sugar

1 egg plus 1 egg white

¼ teaspoon baking soda

¼ teaspoon salt

½ teaspoon xanthan gum

1 teaspoon vanilla

FOR COATING:

3 tablespoons sugar

1 teaspoon cinnamon

1. Preheat oven to 350°F.
2. Mix flour and butter until well combined.
3. Add remaining ingredients. Beat well until batter is quite thick. Set aside.
4. Mix sugar and cinnamon in a small bowl. Stir well.
5. Place rounded teaspoonful of dough on top of sugar mixture. Gently cover with mixture to coat well.
6. Place dough ball (I like to scoop out of sugar mixture with a fork) onto lightly greased baking sheet.
7. Press tops with fingertips or bottom of a glass to flatten just a little.
8. Bake 10–12 minutes, until edges are lightly browned, and cookies are set.
9. Cool on wire racks.

White Chocolate Macadamia Bars

– Brown Rice Flour –
MAKES 12 COOKIE BARS

◆

These bars are a little cakey, a little chewy, and nicely sweet.

¼ cup butter

¾ cup brown rice flour,
95 grams

¾ cup sugar

2 eggs

¼ teaspoon baking soda

¼ teaspoon salt

½ teaspoon xanthan gum

1 teaspoon vanilla

½ cup chopped
macadamia nuts

½ cup white chocolate chips

1. Preheat oven to 350°F.

2. Mix flour and butter until well combined.

3. Add remaining ingredients, except nuts and chips. Beat batter until well combined and thickened. This will help prevent chips or nuts from sinking.

4. Fold in nuts and chips.

5. Pour into 9-inch square baking pan.

6. Bake 15–25 minutes, until edges begin to pull away, and bars test clean with toothpick.

7. Cut into 12 large bars.

CHAPTER 17

Other Desserts

Something a bit sweet at the end of a meal is almost always welcomed by guests. We've grown so accustomed to cakes and cookies that we sometimes forget the many other options we have available to us.

In this chapter I hope to tempt you with alternatives. In particular, I am especially fond of the Poppy Seed Crepes and the Rice Pudding. I tested the crepes with a bit of strawberry jam, which was delicious, but you can fill them with almost anything.

I also suggest you try the Deep Dish Berry Pies recipe. It's lighter than a fully crusted pie but has just enough crust to be interesting.

And, finally, if you are a fan of flan, you should really enjoy the Pumpkin Flan. Just a little cinnamon brings the pumpkin flavor to the forefront. This dessert is understated elegance and very pretty when plated.

Apple Turnovers

– Brown Rice Flour –
MAKES 2 LARGE TURNOVERS

This recipe uses a modification of our pie crust to make it just a hint lighter in texture. I've used Gala apples because they are a little sweet and have nice texture.

PASTRY:

½ cup brown rice flour, 65 grams

2 ounces cream cheese

1 tablespoon sugar

½ teaspoon baking powder

Pinch of salt

¼ teaspoon xanthan gum

⅛ teaspoon baking soda

2 teaspoons water

FILLING:

1 medium apple, finely chopped

¼ teaspoon cinnamon

1 tablespoon sugar

1 teaspoon cornstarch

TOPPING:

1 teaspoon sugar

Sprinkling of cinnamon (optional)

Note: If too much filling is placed on the crust, the crust will break. In this case, less is more. But even if it breaks, it will still be delicious.

1. For the pastry, combine flour and cream cheese. Mix well together to form small crumbs.

2. Add the remaining ingredients and mix well. Working the dough with your hands will help it come together and be more pliable.

3. Roll out dough between two sheets of waxed paper. Roll into 6 x 12-inch rectangle. Cut into two 6-inch squares. Gently place on lightly greased baking sheet.

4. In a small, microwave-safe bowl, combine filling ingredients and mix well. Place in the microwave and cook for 1 minute.

5. Carefully place filling on triangular half of crust (in one of the corners). Fold crust over top and press edges to seal. Cut a few slits in the top to allow steam to escape.

6. Sprinkle tops with sugar (and cinnamon if desired).

7. Bake for 15 minutes, or until fruit is tender, and crust is nicely browned.

Banana Custard Pudding

– Cornstarch –

MAKES 4 ¾-CUP SERVINGS

❖

*This recipe was inspired by just one slightly speckled banana.
It's a wonderful alternative to making banana bread. This recipe was
tested using both almond milk and regular 2 percent milk; both work well.
This is best enjoyed within a day or two of making. Pour the mixture
into a pie shell and top with whipped cream for a special pie too!*

¼ cup sugar

2½ tablespoons cornstarch

½ teaspoon vanilla

2 eggs

2 cups milk (almond or regular)

½ cup pureed banana
(about 1 medium banana)

Pinch of salt

1. Place all ingredients in a medium saucepan. Stir well. A stick blender is especially nice for smoothly blending the banana into the milk.

2. Cook over medium heat, stirring often. Bring to a boil. Mixture should be somewhat thick at this point (it will thicken further while it cools). If not yet thick, cook over heat for an extra minute or so.

3. Pour into individual serving dishes and chill. Serve cold.

Note: Banana baby food also works well in this recipe.

Deep Dish Berry Pies

MAKES 2–4 SERVINGS

◆

Made in two 2-cup ramekins, you'll have an extra pie to share or save for another time. I've used my favorite triple berry (raspberries, blueberries, and blackberries) combination. Any beautiful berry in season can stand alone. These pies are bright in flavor and are just sweet enough.

6 ounces raspberries
(about 1½ cups)

6 ounces blueberries
(about 1½ cups)

6 ounces blackberries
(about 1½ cups)

3½ tablespoons sugar

¼ teaspoon vanilla (optional)

2 tablespoons cornstarch

TOPPING:

Single Pie Crust (page 265)

1 teaspoon sugar

1. Preheat oven to 375°F
2. Prepare pie crust. Set aside.
3. Rinse berries. Drain the berries, but they should be slightly damp.
4. In a medium bowl, combine berries, sugar, vanilla, and cornstarch. Gently mix well.
5. Spray two 2-cup ramekins with nonstick spray. Divide berries between ramekins.
6. Top each ramekin with pie crust. Cut several slits in the crust to allow steam to escape. Sprinkle tops with sugar.
7. Place prepared pies on a baking sheet (to catch juices that may boil over).
8. Bake for 25–30 minutes, until crust is nicely browned, and berries are tender. Juices will be thick and clear.

Individual Fruit Tarts

– Brown Rice Flour –
MAKES 4 FRUIT TARTS

✦

The basis for these tarts is the Rolled Cream Cheese Sugar Cookie recipe (page 248).
I tested three versions of these small tarts to demonstrate how lovely and easy
these tarts are to make. Much to my surprise, cranberry was, by far, my favorite!

½ cup cream cheese

¾ cup brown rice flour,
   95 grams

½ cup sugar

1 egg

¼ teaspoon baking soda

¼ teaspoon salt

½ teaspoon xanthan gum

1 teaspoon vanilla

SUGGESTED TOPPINGS:

- ½ cup fresh cranberries, topped with 1 tablespoon sugar

- 1 pear peeled and sliced, fanned on top of a circle of crust, topped with 1 teaspoon sugar and a sprinkle of nutmeg

- 1 apple peeled and sliced, fanned on top of a circle of crust, topped with 1 teaspoon sugar and a sprinkle of cinnamon

- 1 peach, peeled and sliced, fanned on top of a circle of crust, topped with 1 teaspoon sugar and choice of nutmeg or cinnamon

- 1 plum, peeled and sliced, fanned on top of a circle of crust, topped with 1 teaspoon sugar

- 1 large or 2 small apricots, peeled and sliced, fanned on top of a circle of crust, topped with 1 tablespoon sugar (apricots become more tart during baking)

continued on next page

Other Desserts

257

Individual Fruit Tarts – *continued*

1. Preheat oven to 350°F.

2. Mix flour and cream cheese until well combined.

3. Add remaining ingredients. Beat well. Batter will be thick and tacky.

4. Place dough in the freezer for 30 minutes.

5. Divide dough into 4 parts.

6. Press dough into 4 individual springform tart pans (or make 4-inch circles on a baking sheet).

7. Cover each with the fruit topping of your choice.

8. Bake 25 minutes, until edges are lightly browned, and cookie dough is set and lightly browned.

9. Cool on wire racks.

Pecan Pie

MAKES 8 VERY RICH SERVINGS

*A couple of years ago, I decided to revisit my pecan pie recipe and came up
with a few changes. They include the extra fragrance of the toasted nuts,
a slight molasses flavor, and a toffee undertone from the melted butter.
And, I've chosen to leave some of the nuts whole for a prettier presentation!*

RECOMMENDED CRUST:

Single Pie Crust (page 265)
or your favorite pre-made
pie shell, prebaked for
5–7 minutes.

FILLING:

¼ cup butter

2 cups chopped pecans
(retain several halves
for presentation)

2 tablespoons molasses

4 eggs

1¼ cups brown sugar

¾ teaspoon salt

1 cup light corn syrup,
less 2 tablespoons

1½ teaspoons vanilla

½ teaspoon apple cider vinegar

1. Preheat oven to 425°F.

2. Place butter and nuts in a large
frying pan. Brown over medium
heat, stirring constantly, until
both nuts and butter are fragrant.
Do not burn the butter. Cool to
room temperature.

3. Mix remaining ingredients in a large
bowl. Beat well. Add butter and
pecans. Try to float the pecan halves
on top for a pretty presentation.

4. Bake for 10 minutes. Reduce heat
to 350°F and bake for an additional
45 minutes. A knife inserted in
the middle should test clean.

5. Cool on a wire rack.

Other Desserts

Pie Crust for Pot Pies

– Brown Rice Flour –

This is the crust I used to top the Chicken Pot Pie recipe.
It is also a great small-batch of dough for mini tarts.

½ cup brown rice flour,
 30 grams

2 ounces cream cheese

Pinch of salt

¼ teaspoon xanthan gum

⅛ teaspoon baking soda

2 teaspoons water

1. Preheat oven to 400°F.
2. Combine flour and cream cheese. Mix together to form small crumbs.
3. Add remaining ingredients, and mix well. Working the dough with your hands will help it come together and become more workable.
4. Roll out dough between two sheets of waxed paper and cut as directed, or roll out small circles of dough for mini tarts.

Poppy Seed Crepes

– Brown Rice Flour –
MAKES 4–6 CREPES

*These are delicious with a bit of jam, a little fruit, or even
a splash of chocolate and whipped cream. I was introduced to
this particular crepe with macerated strawberries and a bit of
sour cream on top. Poppy seeds may be omitted for a plain crepe.*

3 eggs

3 tablespoons brown rice flour

2 tablespoons plain
  low-fat yogurt

2 tablespoons milk

Pinch of salt

1 teaspoon sugar

1 tablespoon poppy seeds

Pinch of baking soda

SUGGESTED TOPPINGS
(choose one or more):

- ½ cup of jam
- Fresh berries or other fruits
- Shaved chocolate
- Whipped cream
- Sour cream

1. Combine all ingredients, adding baking soda last. Mix to form smooth, very thin, batter.

2. Heat pan to medium-high. Pour by ¼ cup onto hot, lightly greased pan (nonstick is easiest).

3. Swirl pan to cover bottom of pan with crepe batter. Cook quickly on both sides.

4. Serve warm.

Pumpkin Flan

SERVES 4

*I decided to pair the lovely caramel sauce in a traditional flan
with a bit of pumpkin. And for those of you who cannot tolerate dairy,
I've tested this recipe with almond milk; regular milk would work just fine.
Do not be intimated by a "water bath." Simply place filled custard cups in
a shallow pan and fill pan with water so that the cups have a more even
temperature during baking. This soft flan is creamy and delicious.*

1 cup sugar

4 eggs

¼ cup sugar

1 teaspoon vanilla

1½ cups milk
(almond or regular)

½ cup pumpkin puree

¼ teaspoon cinnamon

1. Preheat oven to 350°F.

2. Place the sugar in a small/medium frying pan (not nonstick). Melt over medium heat, without stirring, until golden in color. (Shake the pan a little to ensure that all the sugar is melted. Do not leave unattended. Turn the heat to low if necessary.) The deeper the color, the deeper the flavor. Do not burn it. CAUTION: that melted sugar is exceedingly hot! Do not touch it with your hands!

3. Place melted sugar in bottoms of 4 1-cup ramekins. (I prefer Pyrex or ceramic for safety.) Set aside.

4. In a medium bowl, combine remaining ingredients, and stir very well with a whisk. (I prefer a stick blender, which will make an ultrasmooth custard.)

5. Place approximately ¾ cup of egg mixture into each ramekin.

6. Place ramekins into a metal baking pan. (I use a full-size cake pan.) Ramekins should be spaced apart. Add enough hot water to pan so that water is approximately half way up the sides of the ramekins. Place in the oven.

7. Bake 50–60 minutes, until knife inserted in the middle of one tests clean.

8. Refrigerate to room temperature or until ready to serve.

9. To plate, run a knife around the top edge of the custard, and cover with a serving saucer. Flip to invert. Remove the ramekin, and sauce will run down the edges of the custard.

Other Desserts

Rice Pudding

SERVES 4

◆◆

This recipe is inspired by an Indian restaurant that my family loves. Cardamom and coconut milk are traditional, but a little cinnamon and whole milk work nicely as well. This dish is not intended to be a solid mass, but rather a gentle creamy dish.

1 14-ounce can coconut milk (not low-fat or light) or 1¾ cups whole milk

1 cup half-and-half

½ cup rice

½ teaspoon vanilla

¼ cup sugar

⅛ teaspoon cardamom or several green cardamom pods or ⅛ teaspoon cinnamon

¼ cup raisins (optional)

1. Combine all ingredients in large saucepan. Stir well.

2. Bring to simmer over medium-low heat. Cook uncovered, stirring often. Do not scorch.

3. Once rice is tender (at least 20 minutes), remove from heat.

4. Serve chilled.

Note: Do not use Jasmine rice in this recipe. I was tempted to do so, given the fragrant and soft nature of the rice, but subsequent testing showed it thickens too much given this formulation. If you cannot resist the urge, however, decrease the amount of rice to ⅓ cup, or increase the amount of milk by at least ½ cup.

Single Pie Crust

– Brown Rice Flour, Sorghum Flour –
MAKES 1 CRUST

◆

*This pie crust is incredibly easy to work with,
even though it will appear to be a bowl of crumbles.
Simply use your hands to knead it into a soft, pliable dough.*

¾ cup brown rice flour,
   95 grams

¼ cup sorghum flour,
   35 grams

4 ounces cream cheese

Pinch of salt

½ teaspoon xanthan gum

¼ teaspoon baking soda

1 tablespoon plus
   1 teaspoon water

1. Preheat oven to 400°F.

2. Combine flour and cream cheese.
   Mix well to form small crumbs.

3. Add remaining ingredients and mix
   well. Working the dough with your
   hands will help it come together and
   become more workable.

4. Roll out dough between two sheets
   of waxed paper. Carefully place into
   pie plate.

5. If using crust as a prebaked shell,
   prick shell once in baking pan, and
   bake for approximately 15 minutes.

6. If filling prior to baking, prick shell
   once in baking pan, and bake for
   about 5 minutes. This will help
   keep the crust from absorbing
   too much moisture from the pie.
   Then continue to bake pie as
   directed.

World's Easiest Peach Crisp

– Brown Rice Flour –
SERVES 5

◆

*Trust me on this one: A little granola, some fresh peaches,
and a few other ingredients combine to create one delicious dessert.
Try it with a scoop of ice cream!*

5 cups sliced peaches (peeled)

1 teaspoon lemon juice

2 tablespoons brown rice flour

2 tablespoons sugar

¼ teaspoon cinnamon

1½ cups gluten-free granola

1. Preheat oven to 350°F.

2. Peel and slice fresh peaches. Place in a large bowl. Toss with lemon juice as you go to avoid browning (or peel faster!).

3. Add remaining ingredients, except granola, and toss well to combine.

4. Pour into a 9-inch square pan or similar casserole dish.

5. Pour granola on top of the peaches.

6. Bake for approximately 20 minutes, until peaches are tender, and juices have thickened.

7. Serve hot or cold.

Gluten-Free Resources

NATIONAL GLUTEN-FREE SUPPORT GROUPS:

American Celiac Society

www.americanceliacsociety.org
PO Box 23455
New Orleans, LA 70183
504-737-3293

Celiac Disease Foundation

www.celiac.org
20350 Ventura Boulevard, Suite 240
Studio City, CA 91364
818-716-1513

Celiac Sprue Association/USA Inc.

www.csaceliacs.org
PO Box 31700
Omaha, NE 68131
877-CSA-4CSA
877-272-4272
402-558-0600

The Gluten Intolerance Group of North America

www.gluten.net
31214 124th Avenue SE
Seattle, WA 98092
253-833-6655

LOCAL CELIAC SUPPORT GROUPS:

Celiac.com

www.celiac.com
Scroll down the home page to locate index, then click on support groups.

GLUTEN-FREE MAIL ORDER SUPPLIERS:

In this book, only a handful of specialty items are necessary. The ingredients used should be readily available to you from your local market or health food store. Listed below are places to order the few items that may not be available locally.

Amazon.com

www.amazon.com

Home to many gluten-free foods and baking supplies! Savings from ordering in quantity; be sure you like the item before you order in bulk. Many gluten-free books can be purchased quite reasonably here as well.

Bob's Red Mill

www.bobsredmill.com
Gluten-free baking supplies and flours.

Celiac.com

www.celiac.com

Home to the "celiac mall," which includes numerous suppliers of gluten-free foods, books, etc.

Clabber Girl

www.clabbergirl.com
Rumford baking powder.

Cream Hill Estates

www.creamhillestates.com
9633 rue Clement
LaSalle, Quebec
Canada H8R 4B4
514-363-2066
1-866-727-3628
Gluten-free oats.

Gifts of Nature, Inc.

www.giftsofnature.net
PO Box 956
Polson, MT 59860
888-275-0003
406-883-3730
Gluten-free oats.

Gluten Free Oats

www.glutenfreeoats.com
578 Lane 9
Powell, WY 82435
888-941-9922
307-754-7041
Gluten-free oats.

MY FAVORITE GLUTEN-FREE BOOK:

Celiac Disease, A Hidden Epidemic, by Dr. Peter Green. Dr. Green takes the reader through the sometimes complicated and intimidating world of gluten-free living. The serious medical content of this book is softened by Dr. Green's straightforward, down-to-earth writing style. The questions and struggles of real patients peppered throughout the work put a human face on the disease.

MY FAVORITE GLUTEN-FREE MAGAZINE:

Living Without
www.livingwithout.com
PO Box 2126
Northbrook, IL 60065

ADDITIONAL RESOURCES FOR THE GLUTEN-FREE COMMUNITY:

In addition to the national and local support groups, www.celiac.com is a wonderful resource for medical studies, recipes, diagnosis steps, etc.

My favorite online discussion board is www.forums.delphi.com/celiac/start. Very importantly, they have adopted a "zero-tolerance" policy for inclusion of any gluten in the diet (i.e., picking croutons off a salad is not safe!). It is a great place to talk with other individuals who live the celiac diet every day. There is no fee for basic membership. You will sometimes find me there.

For vacation getaways without worry, consider www.bobandruths.com.

Note: Thousands of helpful organizations, companies, and websites are available to the gluten-free community. Mountains of information are readily available. After getting safe at home, the next step should be joining a support group—whether national, local, or online—and learning more. And, if you're not the support group type, start learning more by visiting the websites included in this appendix.

METRIC CONVERSIONS

- The recipes in this book have not been tested with metric measurements, so some variations might occur.
- Remember that the weight of dry ingredients varies according to the volume or density factor: 1 cup of flour weighs far less than 1 cup of sugar, and 1 tablespoon doesn't necessarily hold 3 teaspoons.

— General Formulas for Metric Conversion

Ounces to grams	$\Rightarrow$ ounces × 28.35 = grams
Grams to ounces	$\Rightarrow$ grams × 0.035 = ounces
Pounds to grams	$\Rightarrow$ pounds × 453.5 = grams
Pounds to kilograms	$\Rightarrow$ pounds × 0.45 = kilograms
Cups to liters	$\Rightarrow$ cups × 0.24 = liters
Fahrenheit to Celsius	$\Rightarrow$ (°F – 32) × 5 ÷ 9 = °C
Celsius to Fahrenheit	$\Rightarrow$ (°C × 9) ÷ 5 + 32 = °F

— Linear Measurements

½ inch = 1½ cm
1 inch = 2½ cm
6 inches = 15 cm
8 inches = 20 cm
10 inches = 25 cm
12 inches = 30 cm
20 inches = 50 cm

— Volume (Dry) Measurements

¼ teaspoon = 1 milliliter
½ teaspoon = 2 milliliters
¾ teaspoon = 4 milliliters
1 teaspoon = 5 milliliters
1 tablespoon = 15 milliliters
¼ cup = 59 milliliters
⅓ cup = 79 milliliters
½ cup = 118 milliliters
⅔ cup = 158 milliliters
¾ cup = 177 milliliters
1 cup = 225 milliliters
4 cups or 1 quart = 1 liter
½ gallon = 2 liters
1 gallon = 4 liters

— Volume (Liquid) Measurements

1 teaspoon = ⅙ fluid ounce = 5 milliliters
1 tablespoon = ½ fluid ounce = 15 milliliters
2 tablespoons = 1 fluid ounce = 30 milliliters
¼ cup = 2 fluid ounces = 60 milliliters
⅓ cup = 2⅔ fluid ounces = 79 milliliters
½ cup = 4 fluid ounces = 118 milliliters
1 cup or ½ pint = 8 fluid ounces = 250 milliliters
2 cups or 1 pint = 16 fluid ounces = 500 milliliters
4 cups or 1 quart = 32 fluid ounces = 1,000 milliliters
1 gallon = 4 liters

— Oven Temperature Equivalents, Fahrenheit (F) and Celsius (C)

100°F = 38°C
200°F = 95°C
250°F = 120°C
300°F = 150°C
350°F = 180°C
400°F = 205°C
450°F = 230°C

— Weight (Mass) Measurements

1 ounce = 30 grams
2 ounces = 55 grams
3 ounces = 85 grams
4 ounces = ¼ pound = 125 grams
8 ounces = ½ pound = 240 grams
12 ounces = ¾ pound = 375 grams
16 ounces = 1 pound = 454 grams

Index